CW00429776

airline
LIVERIES

GÜNTER ENDRES

Contents

British Library Cataloguing in Publication Data

Endres, Günter G. 1942-
abc Airline Liveries.
I. Title
387.7065

First published 1991

ISBN 0 7110 2025 6

Published by Ian Allan Ltd, Shepperton, Surrey;
and printed by Ian Allan Printing Ltd at their works
at Coombelands in Runnymede, England

Introduction

Today's commercial airlines are distinguishable from other aircraft operators by the colourful designs on their aircraft, visible and recognisable from great distances. There have always been functional elements to the painting of aircraft, though these are perhaps of less importance today than in the very early days when a coat of paint on wood and fabric-covered aircraft provided some modicum of protection from inclement weather. On modern high-speed and high-flying aircraft heat generated by friction and the absorption of the sun's rays – rather than weather – is a problem minimised by light-coloured or white upper fuselages. By contrast, aircraft bellies which are nearer to the runway and get particularly dirty, are usually of grey or darker shades.

The clean shapes of modern jet aircraft have inspired more visually pleasing and highly visible designs, with bands of co-ordinated colour 'cheatlines'

sweeping along the fuselage and up the tailfin, and in some particularly attractive instances, are wrapped around the aircraft. Colours used often reflect those of the national flag, or allude to the airline's purpose. In the latter instance, for example, holiday charter airlines generally favour orange, yellow and blue to represent sun, sand and sky.

Instant recognition of all facets of an airline's operation is today's name of the game. The 'total concept' – that is, full co-ordination of aircraft paint scheme, vehicles, stationery, shops, uniforms and many other items – is now being implemented by virtually every carrier throughout the industry.

There is no doubt that the modern transport aircraft has been turned into the most visible flying advertising hoarding, appearing repeatedly at the numerous regular destinations of the airline's route network.
Günter Endres

dria Airways (JP/ADR)

stablished: 1961
ase: Brnik Airport, Ljubljana, Yugoslavia
ervices: Charter flights to destinations in
Western Europe, North and East Africa,
Middle and Far East, as well as to the
main Yugoslav holiday resorts of Pula,
Split, Zadar, Dubrovnik and Tivat.
International scheduled services from
Ljubljana to Larnaca, Frankfurt, London-
Gatwick, Istanbul, Moscow, Munich,
Paris (with Air France), Vienna and Tel
Aviv.
eet: 1 x Airbus A320-200, 2 x Douglas
DC-9-32, 1 x DC-9-33CF, 2 x de
Havilland Canada DHC-7-100, 1 x
McDonnell Douglas MD-81, 4 x MD-82

On order: 4 x Airbus A320-200
Colour scheme: Large and bold Adria
titles in blue take up half of the clean all-
white fuselage, being highly visible from
a distance. The airline's insignia, which
depicts the initial letter 'A' in blue
reflected in the turquoise waters of the
Adriatic, dominates the tailfin. On the
Airbus A320, the insignia is repeated on
the engine cowlings.
Illustrated: Adria Airways has been
operating Douglas aircraft since its
foundation in 1961 when it started with
DC-6Bs. The latest version in the fleet is
this MD-82 photographed at Cologne.

Aer Lingus (EI/EIN)

Established: 22 May 1936

Base: Dublin Airport, Dublin, Republic of Ireland

Services: European routes from the Irish Republic to Amsterdam, Birmingham, Bristol, Brussels, Copenhagen, Düsseldorf, East Midlands, Edinburgh, Frankfurt, Glasgow, Jersey, Leeds/Bradford, Liverpool, London (Heathrow and Gatwick), Madrid, Manchester, Milan, Paris, Rennes, Rome and Zürich. Transatlantic services are operated to Boston, Chicago and New York. A domestic route system includes Dublin, Connaught Regional, Cork, Galway, Kerry County, Shannon and Sligo.

Fleet: 4 x BAC One-Eleven 200, 3 x Boeing 747-100, 4 x 737-400, 2 x 737-300, 6 x 737-200, 4 x 737-200 Advanced, 3 x 737-200C, 1 x 737-200C Advanced, 4 x Fokker 50, 3 x Shorts 360, 2 x Shorts 360 Advanced

On order: 5 x Boeing 737-500, 1 x 737-400, 1 x Fokker 50

Colour scheme: The livery reflects a bold national identity through an imaginative use of predominantly green colours enhanced with the shamrock insignia. The fuselage displays a light green roof and dark green window cheatline, separated by a narrower band of clear fresh blue. The lower fuselage is divided into white and grey. A large white shamrock adorns the bright green fin. This latest revision of the corporate identity was created by design consultants King & Wetherell.

Illustrated: Aer Lingus operates the Shorts 360 under its Commuter title on domestic services, linking Dublin with some points in the UK.

Aeroflot (SU/AFL)

Established: 9 February 1923

Base: Sheremetievo Airport, Moscow, Soviet Union

Services: Vast domestic network, together with extensive international flights to more than 120 destinations in Europe, Africa, Middle East, Far East and North and Central America. European cities served include Amsterdam, Ankara, Athens, Belgrade, Berlin, Bourgas, Bratislava, Brussels, Budapest, Bucharest, Copenhagen, Dresden, Dublin, Dubrovnik, Düsseldorf, Erfurt, Frankfurt, Gdansk, Geneva, Hamburg, Helsinki, Istanbul, Leipzig, Lisbon, London, Luxembourg, Madrid, Malta, Marseille, Milan, Munich, Nicosia, Oslo, Paris, Prague, Rome, Salzburg, Sofia, Shannon, Stockholm, Tampere, Vienna, Warsaw, Zagreb and Zürich.

Fleet: Antonov An-2, An-12, An-22, An-24, An-26, An-28, An-30, An-32, An-124, An-225, Ilyushin Il-18, Il-62, Il-76, Il-86, LET L-410, Tupolev Tu-134, Tu-154, Yakovlev Yak-40, Yak-42, Yak-72 plus helicopters and specialist aircraft

On order: Ilyushin Il-96-300, Il-114, LET L-610, Tupolev Tu-204, Tu-334

Colour scheme: The standard livery incorporates a dark blue window cheatline fading to a point at front and rear and trimmed by a pinstripe of the same colour below. The upper fuselage and tailfin are in overall white, with the underside in grey. The red Soviet flag dominates the white tail. Aeroflot titling is applied on the front fuselage in mid-blue Cyrillic script, preceded by the airline's winged 'hammer and sickle' insignia.

Illustrated: The 350-seat Ilyushin Il-86 is Aeroflot's only airliner with a widebody cabin. It entered service on 26 December 1980 between Moscow and Tashkent. *Peter J. Cooper*

Aerolineas Argentinas (AR/ARG)

Established: May 1949
Base: Ezeiza Airport, Buenos Aires, Argentina
Services: Extensive scheduled passenger and cargo services throughout the Americas, and across the Atlantic to Frankfurt, London, Madrid, Paris, Rome and Zürich. Trans-Pacific routes link Buenos Aires to Sydney and Auckland. Main domestic services are those between the capital and Cordoba, Mar del Plata and Rosario.
Fleet: 1 x Boeing 707-320B, 8 x 727-200 Advanced, 4 x 737-200, 7 x 737-200C Advanced, 6 x 747-200B, 3 x Fokker F28-1000, 1 x F28-4000
On order: 6 x Boeing 737-500, 2 x 767-300, 1 x McDonnell Douglas MD-87 , 6 x MD-88

Colour scheme: The white-topped fuselage features twin cheatlines in mid and dark blue, extending from the nose and gradually widening along the fuselage. At the fin, each broad cheatline is topped by a similarly coloured and stylised initial 'A'. Dark blue Aerolineas Argentinas titles are carried on the forward fuselage, together with the traditional bird insignia.
Illustrated: All long-haul international services are flown by the Boeing 747-200B which in Aerolineas Argentinas service is fitted out for 399 passengers in a three-class configuration.

Aero Lloyd (YP/AEF)

Established/First Service: 5 December
1980/1 April 1981
Base: Rhein-Main Airport, Frankfurt,
Germany
Services: Passenger charter flights from
various German cities to holiday resorts
in the Mediterranean and the Canary
Islands. Also scheduled domestic
services taking in Frankfurt and Berlin.
Fleet: 3 x McDonnell Douglas DC-9-32, 12
x MD-83, 4 x MD-87
On order: 5 x McDonnell Douglas MD-83,
2 x MD-11

Colour scheme: Bright sunshine shades of
yellow, orange and red cheatlines flow
from the nose to the tail, broken forward
of the wing by bold Aero Lloyd titles in
blue. The triple cheatline is repeated
diagonally across the white fin with the
title riding above. A stylised boxed 'A'
motif appears above the window line
near the front passenger door.
Illustrated: The Aero Lloyd fleet is made
up entirely of McDonnell Douglas twin-
jets and includes this MD-83
photographed at Hamburg. *Udo Weisse
via Browcom*

Air 2000 (DP/AMM)

First service: 11 April 1987
Base: Manchester International Airport, Manchester, UK
Services: Intensive charter programmes from Manchester, London-Gatwick and Glasgow to the principal holiday destinations around the Mediterranean and to Orlando, Toronto, Denver, Mombasa and The Gambia. Among points regularly served are Faro, Lisbon, Malaga, Alicante, Barcelona, Ibiza, Mahon, Palma, Monastir, Malta, Athens, Corfu, Heraklion, Kos, Rhodes, Salonica, Zakynthos, Izmir, Antalya, Dalaman, Larnaca, and Paphos.
Fleet: 12 x Boeing 757-200

Colour scheme: Designed by Marketing Image, the livery comprises red and gold cheatlines under the windows which broaden out along the all-white aircraft and sweep up into the tail. A red Air 2000 logo shaded in gold appears in line on the forward fuselage and stacked on the tailfin. The Rolls-Royce engines have red nacelles with a white horizontal band, on which are superimposed red and gold stripes similar to the fuselage cheatlines. The nacelles also carry gold Rolls-Royce emblems.
Illustrated: From its beginnings with two aircraft, the Rolls-Royce-powered Boeing 757 fleet has grown to 12 in four years. They are configured for 233 passengers.

Air Afrique (RK/RKA)

Established/First Service: March 1961/15
October 1961
Base: Port Bouet Airport, Abidjan, Ivory
Coast
Services: Scheduled passenger and cargo
services throughout Central and West
Africa and to Bordeaux, Casablanca,
Geneva, Lyon, Marseille, Paris, Rome
and Zürich. Also from Abidjan to New
York via Dakar, Senegal.
Fleet: 1 x Airbus A310-300 3 x Airbus
A300B4-200, 1 x McDonnell Douglas
DC-8-55F, 1 x DC-8-63CF, 3 x DC-10-30
On order: 3 x Airbus A310-300

Colour scheme: Broad cheatlines in lime
green and emerald green divide at the
windowline and separate the upper white
fuselage from the grey underside. Bold
Air Afrique titles in a classic black
typeface are displayed on the white roof.
The airline's motif on the tailfin in a
matching emerald green symbolises far
reaching services by the use of a
gazelle's head spanning a stylised globe.
Illustrated: Air Afrique has added the
Airbus A310 to its fleet. It has a total of
four on order for services from West
Africa to Europe.

Air Algerie (AH/DAH)

Established: 1946 as CGTA
Base: Houari Boumedienne Airport, Algiers, Algeria
Services: Scheduled passenger and cargo services to destinations in North and West Africa, Europe and the Middle East. Cities served in Europe include Amsterdam, Athens, Barcelona, Belgrade, Brussels, Bucharest, Frankfurt, Lille, Lyon, London, Madrid, Marseille, Metz, Moscow, Nice, Paris, Prague, Rome, Sofia, Toulouse and Zürich. An extensive domestic network is also operated, together with air taxi and agricultural flying.
Fleet: 1 x Aérospatiale SE3130 Alouette II, 4 x Airbus A310-200, 6 x Beechcraft 65-B80 Queen Air, 2 x Boeing 727-200, 9 x 727-200 Advanced, 13 x 737-200 Advanced, 3 x 737-200C Advanced, 3 x 767-300, 8 x Fokker F27-400M, 3 x Lockheed L382G Hercules

Colour scheme: Introduced in mid-1982, the paint scheme is built around the national colours of red, green and white and features two thin red stripes separated by a broader green band. The upper red cheatline sweeps up and over the rear fuselage into a wide sash. An all-white tail displays the company's red insignia, said to represent its two-letter code 'AH' in the shape of a bird. English and Arabic titles are applied side-by-side on the upper fuselage.
Illustrated: One of Air Algerie's four Airbus A310-200s takes off from Paris-Orly. The aircraft is used to serve destinations in Europe and the Middle East.
Oliver Constant

Air Atlantis (EJ/AIA)

First Service: 1 June 1985

Base: Faro Airport, Faro, Algarve, Portugal

Services: Inclusive-tour charter flights to Portugal from Scandinavia, Ireland, the UK, Belgium, Holland, Germany, France, Switzerland, Austria and Spain. The UK is a major market area, with flights from London-Gatwick, Luton and other regional airports.

Fleet: 3 x Boeing 737-200 Advanced, 4 x 737-300

Colour scheme: A thin red cheatline topped by a broad green stripe (the national colours) runs the whole length of the fuselage below the window line. The company insignia, a stylised 'A' in green and red, is placed centrally on the all-white fin, and repeated to form the first letters in the title on the upper fuselage forward of the wing. The Portuguese flag appears beside the front passenger door.

Illustrated: The Boeing fleet includes four 737-300s which are fitted out for 149 passengers in an all-tourist configuration. This aircraft is pictured at Guernsey collecting Portuguese migrant workers.

Air Bridge (AG/ABR)

Established: November 1972

Base: East Midlands Airport, Castle Donington, Derbyshire, UK

Services: Cargo charter and overnight parcel flights throughout Europe, the Middle East and North Africa. Specialist operator in the transportation of bloodstock and livestock with the Merchantman freighter, which can also accommodate up to 21 accompanying passengers. Also scheduled cargo flights serving Amsterdam, Belfast, Belgrade, Brussels, Cologne, Dublin, Glasgow, London-Heathrow, Luton, Manchester, Shannon, Copenhagen and Stockholm.

Fleet: 3 x Lockheed L188AF/CF Electra, 4 x Vickers V953C Merchantman

Colour scheme: Dramatic black and red lines are wrapped around the nose and sweep along the body of the aircraft. The black cheatline and the white follow-through of the upper fuselage flow diagonally across the predominantly red tailfin. Simple titles in bold black lower case lettering start behind the cargo door. The undersides and wings are finished in pale grey.

Illustrated: Designed as a mainline passenger aircraft in the 1950s, the Lockheed Electra now does an excellent job as a freighter. Air Bridge is currently leasing three to supplement its Merchantman fleet.

Air Canada (AC/ACA)

Established/First Service: 10 April 1937/1
September 1937
Base: Mirabel International Airport,
Montreal, Quebec, Canada
Services: Passenger and cargo services to
the USA, the Caribbean and across the
North Atlantic to Europe. Destinations in
Europe include Düsseldorf, Frankfurt,
Glasgow, London, Manchester, Nice,
Paris, Vienna, Zagreb and Zürich. All
major domestic points are scheduled,
with feeder services provided by six
regional airlines under the 'Air Canada
Connector' network. They are: AirBC,
NWT Air, Air Ontario, Air Toronto, Air
Alliance and Air Nova.
Fleet: 7 x Airbus A320-200, 28 x Boeing
727-200 Advanced, 3 x 747-100, 3 x
747-200, 21 x 767-200, 6 x Lockheed
L1011 TriStar 500, 5 x McDonnell
Douglas DC-8-73, 35 x DC-9-32

On order: 31 x Airbus A320-200, 6 x
Boeing 767-300ER
Colour scheme: A broad warm red band,
extending from above to below the
windows with a narrower burgundy line
underneath, runs the length of the
fuselage, topped by a white roof
incorporating red 'Air Canada' titles. A
similarly warm red tail is dominated by a
maple leaf, the national symbol of
Canada, reversed out in white and
enclosed in a circle. Introduced in 1987,
the new corporate image was designed
by Jack Roberts Marketing Services.
Illustrated: Air Canada's large fleet of
Boeing 767-200s, some of which are
certificated for ETOPS (extended range
twin operations) overwater flights, will
soon be joined by its bigger sister ship,
the 767-300ER.

Air China (CA/CCA)

Established: 2 November 1949
Base: Beijing Capital Airport, Beijing, People's Republic of China
Services: Intercontinental services from Beijing to Karachi, Sharjah, Addis Ababa, Baghdad, Istanbul, Belgrade, Bucharest, Berlin, Rome, Zürich, London, Frankfurt, Paris, Stockholm, Moscow, Vancouver, Toronto, San Francisco, Los Angeles, New York, Sydney and Melbourne. Regional flights to Rangoon, Bangkok, Singapore, Manila, Pyongyang, Osaka, Nagasaki, Fukuoka, and Tokyo. Apart from Beijing, other cities linked into the regional network are Kunming, Guangzhou, Xiamen, Shanghai and Dalian.
Fleet: 5 x Boeing 707-320B/C, 2 x 737-300, 3 x 747-400, 4 x 747-200B/F, 4 x 747SP, 6 x 767-200(ER), 4 x BAe 146-100

On order: 5 x Boeing 747-400, 4 x 767-300
Colour scheme: A white upper fuselage and grey underside are separated by twin mid-blue cheatlines of different width. Black Air China titles in Roman and Chinese characters are preceded by the red national flag incorporating the five-pointed yellow stars. A stylised red phoenix flies on the white tail, said by the Chinese to bring good fortune. On the Boeing 747-400, the phoenix is repeated on the winglets.
Illustrated: Nose-up and side cargo doors enable easy loading of pallets and containers for Air China's first widebody freighter, the Boeing 747-200F, which entered service in November 1990 between Beijing, San Francisco, Los Angeles, Paris and London.

Air France (AF/AFR)

Established: 30 August 1933
Base: Paris Charles de Gaulle Airport,
Roissy, France
Services: Scheduled passenger and cargo
services worldwide, with the exception
of Australia and New Zealand. Extensive
route network within Europe serves
almost 100 destinations plus another 16
in metropolitan France.
Fleet: 4 x Airbus A300B2-100, 11 x
A300B4-200, 7 x A310-200, 3 x A310-
300, 7 x A320-100, 13 x A320-200, 7 x
Aérospatiale/BAe Concorde 100, 10 x
Boeing 727-200, 9 x 727-200 Advanced,
16 x 737-200, 4 x 737-500, 15 x 747-
100, 2 x 747-200, 10 x 747-200B (SCD),
10 x 747-200F, 5 x 747-400

On order: 8 x A320-200, 7 x A340-300, 8 x
Boeing 737-500, 2 x 747-200F, 15 x
747-400/400F
Colour scheme: Based on the French
Tricolour, the pure white overall fuselage
finish is highlighted by bold blue Air
France titles, led by its long established
winged seahorse symbol in blue and red.
The aircraft's major design element is a
splash of colour in the form of blue and
red stripes in varying widths sweeping
up the tailfin. The colour scheme was
introduced in 1975.
Illustrated: Air France has 42 Boeing 747s
in service, with 17 more on order for
delivery in the next three years. This 747-
128 was one of the first to join the fleet in
1970.

Air India (AI/AIC)

Established/First Service: 8 March 1948/8
June 1948
Base: Bombay Airport, Bombay, India
Services: International services from
Bombay, Delhi, Calcutta, Trivandrum and
Madras to destinations in the Far East,
Australia, Middle East, Africa, Europe
and North America. Cities served in
Europe include Frankfurt, Geneva,
London, Moscow, Paris and Rome.
Fleet: 8 x Airbus A310-300, 3 x A300B4-
200, 2 x Boeing 747-300/SCD, 10 x 747-
200B
Colour scheme: Air India selected the sun
for its latest corporate identity unveiled in
October 1989. Shown as a symmetrical
oval, its 24 rays symbolise the 24hrs in a
day. The golden rays and enclosing gold
ring are given added brilliance by a
saffron-yellow outline, a design which
combines the Indian heritage with an
international look. The sun is prominently
positioned on the aircraft against a deep
ambassadorial red sash which extends
from the top of the tail and drapes over a
portion of the all-white fuselage. The Air
India logo is displayed forward in Hindi
and Roman script in red with a metallic
gold shadow.
Illustrated: The A310-300 heads a large
presence of Airbus twin-jets in the
airline's international fleet. Its two-class
configuration seats 29 business and 169
economy class passengers

ir Inter (IT/ITF)

Established/ First Service: 1954/17 March
1958
Base: Orly Airport, Paris, France
Services: Extensive domestic route
network serving 37 destinations in
France, with a main hub at Paris.
Services are divided into five regions:
East and North, South West, West,
South East and Côte d'Azur.
International flights are operated on
behalf of Air France to Porto, Seville,
Malaga, Valence and Venice, together
with seasonal routeings to Ibiza.
Fleet: 19 x Airbus A300B2, 3 x A300B4, 10
x A320-100, 18 x A320-200, 11 x
Dassault Mercure 100
On order: 5 x Airbus A320, 7 x A321, 15 x
A330

Colour scheme: The patriotic red, white
and blue design provides a striking
example of the imaginative use of the
national colours. The clean overall white
fuselage is wrapped at the tail by a light
blue sash flying up the fin, terminating in
red and blue wings. Strong, highly visual
Air Inter titles are applied in blue and red
above the window line. The speed flash
straddles the last letter 'R'.
Illustrated: Air Inter operates a large fleet
of Airbus aircraft, with many more on
order. The A320 illustrated here first
entered service with the French airline in
1988.

AirLanka (UL/ALK)

Established/First Service: 10 January 1979/1 September 1979
Base: Katunyake International Airport, Colombo, Sri Lanka
Services: International scheduled passenger and cargo services from Colombo eastwards to Bangkok, Singapore, Hong Kong, Kuala Lumpur, Fukuoka and Tokyo, and to Trivandrum, Madras, Bombay, Male, Karachi, Dubai, Abu Dhabi, Muscat, Dhahran, Riyadh, Bahrain, Kuwait, Rome, Zürich, Paris, Amsterdam and London.
Fleet: 1 x Airbus A320, 1 x Boeing 737-200, 2 x Lockheed L1011-100/50 TriStar, 3 x L1011-500 TriStar.

Colour scheme: A bright red windowline runs from the nose and spreads out over the entire rear fuselage and tailfin, which forms the backdrop to a large white stylised peacock motif. A thinner red cheatline accompanies the windowline along the whole length of the aircraft. The fuselage is finished in white, with black AirLanka titles in capital letters forward of the wing. The Sri Lankan national flag is applied in front.
Illustrated: AirLanka operates to London-Gatwick from Colombo via Dubai, using its long-range Lockheed TriStar 500. One is seen here about to depart from Gatwick. *Peter J. Cooper*

r Malta (KM/AMC)

Established/First Service: 30 March
1973/1 April 1974
Base: Luqa Airport, Malta
Services: Scheduled passenger and cargo
flights to Amsterdam, Athens, Brussels,
Catania, Frankfurt, Geneva, London
(Heathrow and Gatwick), Lyon, Madrid,
Manchester, Munich, Palermo, Paris,
Rome, Vienna, Zürich and to a number of
North African cities. Geneva and
Palermo are currently served on a
seasonal basis only. Plans for long-haul
services to Australia are a possibility in
1991/92.
Fleet: 1 x Airbus A320-200, 6 x Boeing
737-200A
On order: 1 x Airbus A320-200, 3 x Boeing
737-500

Colour scheme: The Air Malta corporate
symbol is the eight-pointed, four-armed
Maltese Cross. It is displayed in white on
a red field, covering the upper two-thirds
of the tailfin, and underscored by three
solid blue stripes, and repeated on the
engines. The arms of the Maltese Cross
represent the four Christian values of
prudence, justice, fortitude and
temperance, while the three stripes, also
carried along a predominantly white
fuselage, allude to the islands of Malta,
Gozo and Comino. The Air Malta
logotype is applied in a Roman typeface
which complements the basic
characteristics of the Maltese Cross.
This latest corporate identity was
introduced in 1989.
Illustrated: Air Malta began Airbus A320
services to European cities in early
September 1990.

Air Mauritius (MK/MAU)

Established/First Service: 14 June
1967/August 1972
Base: Sir Seewoosagur Ramgoolam
Airport, Plaine Magnien, Mauritius
Services: International and regional flights
to Amsterdam (cargo only),
Antananarivo, Bombay (joint service with
Air India), Durban, Frankfurt (with
Lufthansa), Geneva, Harare, Hong Kong
(with Cathay Pacific), Johannesburg,
Kuala Lumpur, London, Moroni, Munich
(with Lufthansa), Nairobi, Paris, Reunion,
Rodrigues, Rome, Singapore and Zürich.
Fleet: 2 x ATR42-300, 2 x Bell 206B Jet
Ranger, 3 x Boeing 747SP, 2 x 767-
200ER, 1 x DHC-6 Twin Otter 300

Colour scheme: A bright red windowline,
trimmed below with a pinstripe in the
same colour, runs the whole length of
the aircraft, finished in white down to
wing level. Upper case Air Mauritius titles
are promoted alongside the national flag
on the forward fuselage. The airline's red
Paille en Queu (a tropical bird) symbol
flies across a white band on a quartered,
largely red tail.
Illustrated: Two of the airline's three 295-
seat Boeing 747SP-44s photographed in
Mauritius. The ex-South African Airways
aircraft operate all long-haul flights.

Air New Zealand (NZ/ANZ)

Established/First Service: 1939 as
TEAL/30 April 1940

Base: Auckland International Airport,
Auckland, New Zealand

Services: International services from
Auckland, Wellington and Christchurch
across the Tasman Sea to Adelaide,
Brisbane, Cairns, Melbourne, Perth and
Sydney, and to Singapore, Kuala
Lumpur, Bangkok, Nagoya, Bali, Hong
Kong, Tokyo, Nadi, Noumea, Apia,
Tonga, Norfolk Island, Rarotonga,
Papeete, Honolulu, Los Angeles,
Dallas/Fort Worth, Vancouver, Frankfurt
and London. The airline also serves 24
domestic points.

Fleet: 10 x Boeing 737-200 Advanced, 1 x
737-200C Advanced, 5 x 747-200B, 2 x
747-400, 1 x 767-300ER, 8 x 767-200ER,
5 x Fokker F27-100, 10 x F27-500

On order: 6 x Boeing 737-300, 2 x 747-
400, 5 x 767-300

Colour scheme: Air New Zealand's livery,
introduced in 1973, strongly reflects the
mood of its Pacific culture, using the
dazzling blue of the sky, deep turquoise
of the water, together with the bright
silver on it. The twin cheatlines in
turquoise and blue that sweep along the
full length of the upper white and lower
silver metal fuselage, are the lines of the
Polynesian canoe. The largely blue tailfin
edged in turquoise, bears in white the
Koru, a strong, curved spiral that
dominated the beautifully etched canoe
prows. Blue Air New Zealand titles in
lower case on the forward cabin roof are
preceded by the national flag.

Illustrated: Air New Zealand's international
fleet is headed by the Boeing 747, the
first of which was delivered in May 1981.
The 747-200B depicted here, has since
been joined by the latest -400 model.

Air Seychelles (HM/SEY)

Established: 15 September 1977
Base: Seychelles International Airport, Victoria, Mahe, Seychelles
Services: International passenger services from Mahe to Mauritius, Singapore, Frankfurt, Paris, Rome and London-Gatwick. Also domestic inter-island flights between Mahe, Praslin, Fregate, Bird and Denis.
Fleet: 1 x Boeing 767-200ER, 2 x DHC-6 Twin Otter 300, 1 x Dornier Do228-200, 2 x Britten-Norman BN-2A Islander
Colour scheme: A pair of pure white fairy terns flying in harmony against the background of the red and green colours of the Seychelles flag, is the airline's symbol applied to the tailfin of its aircraft. The lower green is preceded by three graduated diagonal stripes wrapped over the top of the all-white fuselage. Blue Air Seychelles titles are displayed on the upper fuselage, together with the national flag. The symbol is also applied to the natural metal finish of the engine cowlings.
Illustrated: Flagship of the fleet is the Boeing 767-200ER which flies the airline's intercontinental service to Frankfurt, Paris, Rome and London.

Airtours International

Established/First Service: 1990/March
1991

Base: Manchester International Airport,
Manchester, UK

Services: Inclusive-tour services to
Europe and the Mediterranean holiday
resorts, as well as further afield to the
Caribbean, Mexico, USA and Kenya from
London-Gatwick and Stansted,
Birmingham, Cardiff, East Midlands,
Glasgow, Liverpool, Manchester and
Newcastle

Fleet: 5 x McDonnell Douglas MD-83

Colour scheme: This unusual livery is
distinguished by a combination of light
and dark blue supporting the white
upper fuselage. The dark blue tail
incorporates the initial 'A' on a light blue
sun and then extends downwards and
along the full length of the aircraft belly.
Streamlining is effected by a single green
pinstripe set into the top of the dark blue
underside, and three of varying lengths
running along the leading edge of the fin.
Blue Airtours titles appear forward of the
wing under the windows. The Airtours
flying colours were created by London
design group LLE/H.

Illustrated: The McDonnell Douglas MD-
83s are busy carrying holidaymakers to
many exotic destinations.

Air UK/Air UK Leisure (UK/UKA)

Established: 16 January 1980
Base: London-Stansted Airport, Stansted, Essex, UK
Services: Scheduled passenger services within the UK and to Europe, serving Aberdeen, Amsterdam, Belfast, Bergen, Brussels, Edinburgh, Glasgow, Guernsey, Humberside, Jersey, Leeds/Bradford, London (Heathrow, Gatwick and Stansted), Newcastle, Norwich, Paris (Charles de Gaulle), Southampton, Stavanger and Teesside. Air UK Leisure, founded in 1987 as a sister company, started operations on 30 April 1988 serving the European leisure market.
Fleet: 2 x BAe 146-100, 3 x 146-200, 4 x 146-300, 11 x Fokker F27-200, 2 x F27-500, 3 x F27-600/F, 2 x Shorts 360
On order: Air UK: 5 x BAe 146-100, 2 x 146-300
Air UK Leisure: 4 x Boeing 737-400
On order: 3 x 737-400
Colour scheme: Triple route bands in three shades of blue, unusually rounded at the beginning and starting at different points, run along the all-white fuselage, narrowing at the rear to a single dark blue line which sweeps up the tail to form the 'mast' on which flutters a half union flag. Air UK titles in a classic Perpetua Bold typeface behind the forward passenger door are underlined by a red pinstripe which continues on to the rear where it merges with the cheatlines. The Air UK Leisure scheme differs only by the addition of the word 'Leisure' after Air UK in red handwriting. The livery, introduced in 1987, was designed by UK company Dan Ranger Associates.
Illustrated: Air UK operates all three versions of the British Aerospace four-engined 146 jetliner, including these 146-300s pictured at Innsbruck. Air UK Leisure became the first airline outside the USA (and second overall) to operate the Boeing 737-400, when it took delivery of its first aircraft on 15 October 1988.

Air Zimbabwe (UM/AZW)

Established: 1 September 1967 as Air Rhodesia

Base: Harare Airport, Harare, Zimbabwe

Services: Long-haul services to Sydney via Perth and to European destinations including London-Gatwick, Frankfurt, and Athens via Larnaca. The airline also flies regional routes in Southern and East Africa, serving Durban, Johannesburg, Gaborone, Manzini, Maputo, Lusaka, Nairobi, Lilongwe, Dar-es-Salaam and Mauritius, together with an eight-point domestic network.

Fleet: 4 x Boeing 707-320B (being phased out), 3 x 737-200 Advanced, 2 x 767-200ER, 1 x BAe 146-200

Colour scheme: A quadruple cheatline of the national colours of green, yellow, red and black on a white upper fuselage, produces an exciting colour scheme. Commencing at the nose, the stripes step up in broader diagonal bands to the windowline, ultimately embracing most of the tailfin. Near the top of the fin appears the Zimbabwe bird, a soapstone carving of an ancient African culture, fronting the red star of socialism and national aspiration. Air Zimbabwe titles are displayed alongside a fluttering portrayal of the national flag.

Illustrated: The Boeing 707-320B is being phased out in favour of the twin-engined Boeing 767. *Peter J. Cooper*

Alitalia/ATI (AZ/AZA)

Established/First Service: 16 September
1946/May 1947
Base: Leonardo da Vinci Airport, Rome,
Italy
Services: International passenger and
cargo services to more than 100 cities in
50 countries on all continents. Also
extensive domestic services in its own
colours and those of Aero Transporti
Italiani (ATI), a wholly-owned subsidiary
based at Naples.
Fleet: 15 x Airbus A300B4-100/200, 9 x
ATR42-300, 12 x Boeing 747-
200B/(SCD), 1 x 747-200F, 42 x
McDonnell Douglas DC-9-32, 58 x MD-
82, 4 x McDonnell Douglas MD-11C
On order: 20 x Airbus A321, 6 x McDonnell
Douglas MD-11C, 8 x MD-82, 25 x MD-
87
Colour scheme: A striking corporate
image using the national colours of red,
white and green. Designed by Walter

Landor Associates and adopted
fleetwide in January 1971, it focuses on
a simple, yet bold stylised 'A' in green
with a red centre, which fills the tailfin as
a continuation of a green windowline.
The 'A' is repeated as the first letter in
the black italic logotype on the all-white
fuselage. The ATI livery is closely based
on Alitalia's, but the colours are dark
blue and light blue. Additionally, the
windowline is foreshortened to allow the
application of its logo which takes up a
large part of the forward fuselage.
Illustrated: Alitalia's MD-80 fleet will
number 97 aircraft by the end of 1996,
by which time the earlier DC-9s will have
been phased out. The McDonnell
Douglas twinjets are frequently
interchanged with ATI, which also
operates nine of the ATR42-300 regional
aircraft fitted out for 48 passengers.

All Nippon Airways (ANA) (NH/ANH)

Established: December 1957

Base: Narita Airport, Tokyo, Japan

Services: Comprehensive domestic network linking 30 major cities on all Japanese islands with high-frequency services. Since 1986 also international routes now serving Guam, Saipan, New York, Los Angeles, Washington, Beijing, Dalian, Hong Kong, Seoul, Bangkok, Singapore, Sydney; and London, Stockholm, Paris, Moscow and Vienna in Europe.

Fleet: 3 x Boeing 737-200, 11 x 737-200 Advanced, 5 x 747-200B, 2 x 747-200F, 17 x 747SR, 1 x 747-400, 25 x 767-200, 18 x 767-300, 11 x Lockheed L1011 TriStar 1, 9 x NAMC YS-11

On order: 20 x Airbus A320-200, 42 x Boeing 747-400, 27 x 767-300

Colour scheme: An angular cheatline in two shades of blue broadens along the white upper fuselage until it takes over the whole of the tail, incorporating the 'ANA' logo in white. The logo also appears in Japanese on both sides of the fuselage near the front passenger door and is preceded by the *hi-no-maru* – or sun disk – of the national flag. The livery was introduced in 1983 with the delivery of the Boeing 767s.

Illustrated: The Boeing-dominated fleet includes the Boeing 747-200B, one of which is seen here landing at London-Gatwick Airport.

American Airlines (AA/AAL)

Established: 13 May 1934

Base: Dallas/Fort Worth Airport, Fort Worth, Texas, USA

Services: Comprehensive domestic network right across USA, including feeder services by a number of regional airlines under the banner of 'American Eagle'. Also international schedules to Canada, Mexico, the Caribbean and Japan, and since 1982 across the Atlantic to Europe, now serving London, Düsseldorf, Frankfurt, Geneva, Madrid, Manchester, Munich, Paris and Zürich.

Fleet: 25 x Airbus A300-600R, 29 x Boeing 727-100, 125 x 727-200 Advanced, 2 x 747SP, 20 x 757-200, 30 x 767-200/ER, 15 x 767-300ER, 6 x BAe146-200A, 48 x McDonnell Douglas DC-10-10/ER, 9 x DC-10-30, 170 x MD-82, 10 x MD-83

On order: 6 x Airbus A300-600R, 30 x Boeing 757-200, 25 x 767-200, 10 x 767-300ER, 75 x Fokker 100, 15 x McDonnell Douglas MD-11, 70 x MD-82.

Colour scheme: A highly-polished natural metal fuselage and tail finish provides the backdrop for a 'straight-through' patriotic triple cheatline in red, white and blue. The long-established motif of a blue eagle swoops down between the twin peaks of the double red and blue 'A' initials, outlined in white. 'American' lettering in red, again with a white outline, is displayed on the cabin roof. The livery was adopted in 1969.

Illustrated: The McDonnell Douglas DC-10, one of the types used across the North Atlantic, is one of several aircraft which were developed with important contributions from this long-established American carrier.

Aurigny Air Services: (GR/AUR)

Established: 1 March 1968

Base: States Airport, Alderney, Channel Islands

Services: Frequent scheduled passenger and freight flights within the Channel Islands, linking the three main islands of Jersey, Guernsey and Alderney. Also schedules to Cherbourg and Dinard in northern France from Guernsey and Jersey, and from Alderney to Southampton and Bournemouth, as well as mail and newspaper flights into Alderney, and between Guernsey and Jersey.

Fleet: 9 x Pilatus (Britten-Norman) BN-2A Mk III Trislander, 1 x Shorts 360

Colour scheme: Aurigny's aircraft feature a striking bright yellow overall colour scheme with red and black cheatlines along the fuselage. These are interrupted by the word 'Aurigny', which is the old French name for the airline's home base of Alderney, stencilled in large, bold black lettering. Displayed on the tailfin is the rampant lion of Alderney in red with white detail.

Illustrated: The Britten-Norman Trislander forms the mainstay of Aurigny's fleet of 'yellowbirds'. With the very short sector times between the islands, each Trislander has to make some 3,500-4,000 take-offs and landings each year.

Austrian Airlines (OS/AUA)

Established/First Service: 30 September 1957/31 March 1958
Base: Schwechat Airport, Vienna, Austria
Services: Scheduled passenger and cargo services throughout Europe, to Baghdad, Damascus, Jeddah, Riyadh and Tehran in the Middle East, Tokyo, and across the North Atlantic to New York. The airline has a good coverage of Eastern Europe, serving Moscow, Kiev, Leningrad, Berlin, Prague, Warsaw, Budapest, Sofia and Bucharest. Domestic services linking Vienna, Graz, Innsbruck, Salzburg and Klagenfurt, are operated by its subsidiary, Austrian Air Services with Fokker 50 aircraft.
Fleet: 2 x Airbus A310-300, 11 x McDonnell Douglas MD-81, 2 x MD-82, 2 x MD-87ER, 3 x MD-87SR
On order: 2 x Airbus A310-300, 6 x A320-200, 7 x A321, 2 x McDonnell Douglas MD-87ER

Colour scheme: Basically unchanged since Austrian's foundation in 1957, the red, white, red tailfin arrangement underlines its national identity, and this is complemented by simple Austrian titles and a large chevron 'wing' insignia in the same red on the forward cabin. The aircraft are named after Austrian provinces and towns and these names, together with the crest, can be found below the cockpit on the now all-white fuselage.
Illustrated: Flagship of the fleet is the Airbus A310 which entered service on 9 January 1989 on the Vienna-Istanbul route, and was subsequently put on the long-haul New York and Tokyo services. *Prof Johannes Zopp*

Avianca (AV/AVA)

Established: 5 December 1919 as SCADTA

Base: Eldorado International Airport, Bogota, Colombia

Services: Extensive domestic network and scheduled flights throughout Latin America, Caribbean, the USA and Europe. Destinations include Frankfurt, Madrid, Paris, Miami, New York, Los Angeles, Cancun, Guatemala City, San José, Panama City, Mexico City, Aruba, Curaçao, Port-au-Prince, Santo Domingo, Caracas, Quito, Lima, Rio de Janeiro, Buenos Aires, Montevideo and Santiago de Chile.

Fleet: 3 x Boeing 707-320B, 15 x 727-100, 1 x 727-200, 8 x 727-200 Advanced, 1 x 747-100, 1 x 747-200B(SCD), 2 x 767-200ER

On order: 1 x Boeing 767-200ER

Colour scheme: The upper half of the fuselage is painted in a warm red, falling away from a complete coverage at the nose to above the window-line at the rear and continuing up the back of the tail. Avianca Colombia titles are set into the red field in white and black respectively. Red Avianca lettering colours the white section of the fin.

Illustrated: The latest addition to Avianca's fleet is the Boeing 767-200ER, delivered during 1990.

Balkan Bulgarian Airlines (LZ/LAZ)

Established/First Service: 29 June
1947/12 September 1947
Base: Vrajdebna Airport, Sofia, Bulgaria
Services: Domestic and international
passenger and cargo services to points
in Europe, Africa and the Middle and Far
East. European destinations, served from
Sofia, include Amsterdam, Ankara,
Athens, Barcelona, Belgrade, Berlin,
Bratislava, Brussels, Bucharest,
Budapest, Copenhagen, Dresden,
Frankfurt, Helsinki, Istanbul, Kiev,
Larnaca, Leningrad, London, Madrid,
Malta, Milan, Moscow, Paris, Prague,
Rome, Stockholm, Vienna, Warsaw and
Zürich.
Fleet: 4 x Antonov An-12, 1 x An-24RV, 15
x An-24V, 2 x Boeing 737-500, 2 x
Ilyushin Il-18D, 4 x Il-18V, 8 x Mil Mi-8, 5
x Tupolev Tu-134, 11 x Tu-134A/-3, 14 x
Tu-154B/-1/-2, 6 x Tu-154M, 9 x
Yakovlev Yak-40

On order: 1 x Boeing 737-500
Colour scheme: Narrow twin cheatlines in
the national colours of red and mid-
green flow along the pure white fuselage
wrapping around the belly of the aircraft
behind the wing. Red and green brush
strokes on the white tail add a fresh,
modern look. Bold red Balkan titles are
applied in English on the starboard side
and Bulgarian on port, midway on the
cabin roof behind the 'shooting star'
emblem. These are followed by smaller
Bulgarian Airlines sub-titles in green. The
present scheme was adopted in late
1985.
Illustrated: The Ilyushin Il-18, first
introduced into service in 1962, remains
a familiar sight at European airports. Six
105-seat Il-18s remain in regular service
Peter Zsillé

Biman Bangladesh Airlines (BG/BBC)

Established/First Service: 4 January
1972/February 1972
Base: Zia International Airport, Dhaka,
Bangladesh
Services: Scheduled international services
from the capital Dhaka to Kuala Lumpur,
Singapore, Bangkok, Yangon,
Kathmandu, Calcutta, Bombay, Karachi,
Dubai, Abu Dhabi, Kuwait, Muscat,
Doha, Dhahran, Jeddah, Tripoli, Athens,
Rome, Amsterdam and London. Also
domestic flights to seven major cities.
Fleet: 3 x BAe ATP, 3 x Fokker F27-600
Friendship, 2 x F28-4000 Fellowship, 4 x
McDonnell Douglas DC-10-30

Colour scheme: The national colours of
red and dark green are used in the form
of a cheatline running at window level
the whole length of the all-white
fuselage. Black titles are carried in
English and Bengali on the port and
starboard side respectively. A white
stork, flying across the setting sun, is
positioned centrally between horizontal
fin bands in red and green. The livery
was introduced in 1983.
Illustrated: The BAe ATP airliner is the
latest addition to the fleet, the first being
handed over in August 1990. The three
aircraft are operated on the domestic
network and to neighbouring countries.

Birmingham European Airways (BEA) (VB/BEX)

Established/First Service: January 1983/8 June 1983

Base: Birmingham International Airport, Birmingham, UK

Services: Scheduled international services from Birmingham to European destinations including Amsterdam, Copenhagen, Cork, Düsseldorf, Milan, Stockholm and Stuttgart. Cross-country connections are provided to Newcastle in the northeast and to Belfast in Northern Ireland.

Fleet: 5 x BAC One-Eleven-400, 3 x Gulfstream I

Colour scheme: Smart silver-grey Birmingham European titles on the cabin roof complement similarly coloured diagonal stripes of varying widths wrapped around the rear of the all-white fuselage. A broad light blue band separates the silver grey from the deep blue which covers the tailfin, rear fuselage and engines. The 'BEA' logo is reversed out of the deep blue in white, with the centre part of the 'E' finished in light blue. The livery was introduced in 1990 with the delivery of the One-Elevens.

Illustrated: One-Eleven 416EK, G-AWBL, seen here landing at Birmingham, is one of five ex-British Airways aircraft introduced during 1990. They are operated in a 74-seat configuration.

Brit Air (DB/BZH)

Established: 1973

Base: Ploujean Airport, Morlaix, Brittany, France

Services: Scheduled regional services within France, linking Le Havre, Caen, Rennes, Brest, Lyon, Quimper and Toulouse, and cross-border services to London-Gatwick from Le Havre, Caen and Brest. Seasonal flights to Cork from Brest and Nantes. Also flights on behalf of Air France from Paris to other destinations in Europe.

Fleet: 2 x ATR72, 10 x ATR42-300, 2 x Beech Super King Air 200, 1 x Piper PA-31T Cheyenne II, 6 x Saab 340A

Colour scheme: The tailfin features a linear design in yellow and dark blue pinstriping, emanating from low-level cheatlines starting at the nose. Brit Air titles are applied near the front, together with the company symbol, either above the cheatlines or set within. The symbol, also in yellow and dark blue, represents 'Triskell' and 'Hermine', emblems of Brittany.

Illustrated: Brit Air's schedules are shared by the Saab 340, ATR-300 fitted out for 42 passengers (pictured here), and its larger 68-passenger sister ship, the ATR72.

Britannia Airways (BY/BAL)

Established/First Service: 1 December
1961/5 May 1962
Base: Luton Airport, Luton, Bedfordshire,
UK
Services: Inclusive-tour charter flights
from Luton, London-Gatwick,
Manchester and some 20 other
provincial UK airports to more than 100
regular destinations throughout Europe
and the Mediterranean countries, taking
in all the main holiday resort areas of
Portugal, Spain, Italy, Yugoslavia,
Greece, Turkey, Tunisia, Morocco, the
Canary Islands, Madeira and Malta. Also,
long-haul routes are operated to such
destinations as The Gambia in West
Africa, Australia, New Zealand, Mexico,
the United States and the Caribbean.
Fleet: 3 x Boeing 767-200, 5 x 767-200ER,
6 x 737-300, 19 x 737-200 Advanced, 4
x 737-200, 2 x 757-200

On order: 6 x Boeing 767-200ER, 4 x 757-
200
Colour scheme: A patriotic livery with
deep-blue full-length stripes beginning a
the belly of the aircraft and graduating to
a pinstripe as they approach the window
line. The blue is trimmed with narrow red
and gold bands. The white upper
fuselage displays strong Britannia
lettering and Britannia's helmeted head
in blue outlined in red. She carries a
trident and holds the Union flag shield,
sitting on the blue tail above reversed
pinstripes. The livery was created by
London design house Peter Eaton and
Partners and implemented in 1983.
Illustrated: Flagship of the fleet is the
Boeing 767-200ER, first delivered to the
airline in February 1984. Powered by two
General Electric CF6-80A turbofans, the
aircraft can be used on extended-range
overwater operations.

British Air Ferries (BAF)

Established: January 1963

Base: Southend Airport, Southend-on-Sea, Essex, UK

Services: Passenger and cargo charter and contract services throughout the UK and Europe, including sub-services for other airlines, IT flights, and regular routeings for Shell between Aberdeen and Sumburgh. Also express freight services on behalf of Securicor, for Federal Express between Dublin, Birmingham and Brussels and newspaper flights to various destinations including Malta.

Fleet: 12 x Vickers V800 Viscount, 2 x V800C Freightmaster, 1 x BAe 146-200QC, 2 x BAC One-Eleven 200, 3 x Handley Page HPR7 Herald 200, 1 x Fokker F27-200 (owned by Federal Express)

Colour scheme: After a brief diversion (see photograph) the airline is reverting to its previous colour scheme which features the blue 'BAF' logo on the white tail underscored by a broadened continuation of the patriotic red and blue pinstripes along the fuselage. These cheatlines provide the transition from the white upper fuselage to the midnight blue lower body of the aircraft. British Air Ferries titles in blue and red on the cabin roof are preceded by the Union flag. The livery was designed by David Taylor and Mike Kay in 1985.

Illustrated: The large BAF fleet of Vickers Viscount turboprop aircraft is undergoing a life-extension programme which should keep the aircraft in service for another 15 years.

British Airways (BA/BAW)

Established: 31 March 1924 as Imperial
Airways/1 April 1972
Base: London-Heathrow Airport,
Hounslow, Middlesex, UK
Services: The largest global network of
scheduled passenger and cargo services
linking the UK with 150 cities in 75
countries on all continents. Also a
comprehensive domestic network
including the main 'Super Shuttle'
services from London to Manchester,
Glasgow, Edinburgh and Belfast, the
Scottish Highlands and Islands routes
and regional flights.
Fleet: 7 x Aérospatiale/BAC Concorde, 10
x Airbus A320-200, 43 x Boeing 737-
200, 4 x 737-300, 16 x 747-100, 20 x
747-200B/(SCD), 15 x 747-400, 36 x
757-200, 5 x 767-300ER, 34 x BAC One-
Eleven 500, 9 x BAe (HS) 748, 8 x BAe
ATP, 5 x Lockheed L1011 TriStar
1/50/100, 8 x L1011 TriStar 200, 8 x
McDonnell Douglas DC-10-30
On order: 27 x Boeing 737-300/400/500,
27 x 747-400, 14 x 767-300ER
Colour scheme: The British Airways

corporate identity was designed by
Walter Landor Associates and unveiled
in December 1984. It has been designed
around three colours: pearl grey, rich
midnight blue and Speedwing red. The
Speedbird emblem, in use since the
days of Imperial Airways, was the
inspiration behind the dramatic red
Speedwing, which provides an essential
link between the nose and the fin of the
aircraft and forms a close relationship
with the stylised Union Jack.
The tailfin is divided into two halves, with
the upper in midnight blue promoting the
coat of arms in grey above a quartered
Union Jack, set into the lower pearl grey
The British Airways titles, in a bold
Optima typeface, are traditionally placed
and aligned with the red Speedwing,
which runs almost the full length of the
fuselage, providing a bold separation
between the pearl grey top and midnight
blue lower fuselage and engine nacelles.
Aircraft registrations and names are
highlighted in grey against the blue.
Slight variations exist within the

British Midland Airways (BD/BMA)

Established: 1964

Base: East Midlands Airport, Castle Donington, Derbyshire, UK

Services: Scheduled passenger services from London-Heathrow Airport and East Midlands Airport to Amsterdam, Belfast, Birmingham, Brussels, Dublin, Edinburgh, Glasgow, Liverpool, Leeds/Bradford, Paris, Teesside and the Channel Islands. Applications are pending for a number of new European routes.

Fleet: 6 x Boeing 737-300, 3 x 737-400, 3 x BAe ATP, 4 x DHC7-100, 6 x McDonnell Douglas DC-9-14/15, 8 x DC-9-32

Colour scheme: A narrow white cheatline separates the pale grey underside of the aircraft from the blue cabin roof. British Midland titles in upper and lower case lettering are applied alongside the red 'BM' motif which is partially striated to give the appearance of speed. The 'M' is crowned with a blue diamond, alluding to the airline's in flight Diamond Service. The livery was unveiled in October 1985.

Illustrated: The Boeing 737-300, together with the -400 Series, heads the short-to-medium range fleet used both domestically and across Europe. G-OBMA was the first 737-300 to enter service, on lease from Ansett Worldwide Aviation Services.

Concorde Fleet. Concorde has an equally distinctive all-white fuselage in order to reflect the heat and keep to a minimum the extremely high surface temperatures generated in supersonic flight.

The coat of arms was granted to British Airways in January 1975, in recognition of its service to the nation. Prepared by York Herald of Arms, Dr Conrad Swan, it was inspired in part by the Union Jack which is recognised universally as the national flag. The shield is supported by Pegasus, the winged horse, and a lion guardant winged at the shoulders. Above the shield is the helm and crest, consisting of a sunburst symbolic of energy, strength and vitality, rising from an astral crown. The motto is 'To Fly to Serve'.

Illustrated: British Airways' seven Concorde airliners completed 15 years of successful service on 26 January 1991. In contrast, the high technology fly-by-wire 150-seat Airbus A320 did not enter service until 29 April 1988. Ten of this popular twinjet are now in service.

Brymon Airways (BC/BRY)

Established: 15 June 1972
Base: Plymouth City Airport, Crownhill, Plymouth, Devon, UK
Services: Scheduled passenger services linking London-Heathrow to the West Country points of Plymouth and Newquay; London-Gatwick to Plymouth and Exeter; London-City Airport to Paris, and for Air France to Lille and Strasbourg; and Bristol to Glasgow, Edinburgh, Dublin, Plymouth and Paris. The Channel Islands and Cork also have leisure services from Plymouth.
Fleet: 7 x DHC7-100, 2 x DHC8-100, 1 x DHC-6 Twin Otter 300

On order: 4 x DHC8-300
Colour scheme: A broad bright yellow band leading two narrower grey and blue stripes are wrapped around the rear part of the white fuselage, taking over most of the tailfin. A rhombus of the same colours is repeated on the engine cowlings. Black italic Brymon lettering appears on the lower forward fuselage and up the yellow part of the tail.
Illustrated: The twin-engined Boeing de Havilland DHC8-100 is the latest addition to Brymon's fleet of STOL aircraft from the same manufacturer.

BWIA International (BW/BWA)

Established: 27 November 1939
Base: Piarco Airport, Port of Spain, Trinidad and Tobago
Services: Passenger and cargo flights throughout the Caribbean islands and to Caracas, Baltimore, Miami, New York and Toronto. Trans-Atlantic services link Port of Spain with Frankfurt, London and Zürich.
Fleet: 4 x Lockheed L1011 TriStar 500, 2 x McDonnell Douglas DC-9-51, 8 x MD-83
Colour scheme: A golden 'sand' cheatline above a Caribbean blue sky pinstripe

flows up the tailfin and is interrupted by the company's sun symbol in turquoise and gold, broken by magenta BWIA initials. Trinidad and Tobago Airways and BWIA International titles cover the entire forward fuselage, either side of the national flag. The lettering is in black with the exception of BWIA which is again in magenta.
Illustrated: The Lockheed TriStar 500 flies all the airline's long-haul services. the first of four aircraft was delivered at the end of January 1980. *Peter J. Cooper*

Caledonian Airways (KT/BKT)

Established: 10 December 1987

Base: London-Gatwick Airport, Crawley, West Sussex, UK

Services: Holiday charters to the traditional Mediterranean market, plus long-haul flights to destinations as far afield as Barbados, Jamaica, the Dominican Republic, the USA and Kenya. Among the most frequent destinations are Malaga, Alicante, Gerona, Murcia, together with the island points of Mahon, Palma and Ibiza in the Balearics, and Corfu, Heraklion, Chania, Keffalonia, Zakynthos, Skiathos, Mykonos, Kos, Athens and Salonika in Greece. Many other resorts are also served in Portugal, Morocco, Tunisia, Italy, Yugoslavia, Turkey and the Canary Islands.

Fleet: 5 x Boeing 757-200 (ER), 6 x Lockheed L1011-1 TriStar

Colour scheme: The Caledonian Airways fleet combines the best of both British Airways and the former British Caledonian Airways. The fuselage features the pearl grey upper and midnight blue underside of the former with the red speedwing replaced by a narrow gold cheatline. The tailfin displays the familiar 'Lion Rampant' of BCal in the standard blue and gold arrangement. The word Caledonian is reproduced on the cabin roof in the same Optima typeface as British Airways.

Illustrated: The Caledonian fleet is headed by five ETOPS (extended range twin operations) equipped Boeing 757-200s which enable the airline to fly overwater, provided it is no further than 138min from a diversionary airfield should one engine fail.

Canadian Airlines International (CP/CDN)

Established: 31 January 1942
Base: Calgary International Airport, Calgary, Canada
Services: Extensive domestic and regional flights together with long-haul services to Auckland, Bangkok, Beijing, Buenos Aires, Copenhagen, Frankfurt, Hong Kong, Honolulu, Lima, London, Los Angeles, Manchester, Mexico City, Milan, Munich, Nagoya, Nadi, Paris, Rio de Janeiro, Rome, San Juan, San Francisco, Santiago de Chile, Sao Paulo, Sydney and Tokyo.
Fleet: 12 x Airbus A310-300, 60 x Boeing 737-200 Advanced, 1 x Boeing 747-400, 10 x 767-300ER, 4 x McDonnell Douglas DC-10-30, 7 x DC-10-30ER
On order: 18 x Airbus A320-200, 2 x Boeing 747-400, 2 x 767-300ER.

Colour scheme: The midnight blue belly of the aircraft is separated from the white cabin roof by 'straight-through' pinstripe red and 'pewter' cheatlines. The latter matches the expanded tail bars, which represent the five continents served and form the backdrop to the red wing symbol, formerly of Pacific Western. The cabin roof displays Canadian titles in black, with the penultimate character replaced by the company insignia, so that it can be read as either Canadian or the French Canadien, without having to apply dual titling.
Illustrated: Canadian Airlines uses its Boeing 767-300ERs on ETOPS across the North Atlantic. Its 767s are powered by two General Electric CF6-80C2 turbofan engines.

Cargolux (CV/CLX)

Established: 4 March 1970
Base: Findel Airport, Luxembourg
Services: Regular all-cargo services between Europe, the Middle East, Asia, Canada and the USA. Specialisation in the carriage of general cargo, sensitive freight, perishables, livestock, outsize cargo and dangerous goods. Also maintenance and leasing services.
Fleet: 3 x Boeing 747-200F, 1 x 747-100 (leased out)
On order: 3 x Boeing 747-400F

Colour scheme: The fuselage, painted overall in light-grey, is highlighted by simple straight cheatlines using the blue, white and red tricolour of Luxembourg, broken on the forward fuselage by bold black cargolux titling in lower case lettering. The airline's distinctive three-dimensional 'triple-box' motif in red outlined in white, dominates the aircraft's massive tailfins.
Illustrated: Cargolux's fleet of Boeing 747-200Bs will soon be joined by three of the larger 747-400F model.

Cathay Pacific Airways (CX/CPA)

Established: 24 September 1946
Base: Kai Tak International Airport, Hong Kong
Services: Scheduled passenger and cargo services to destinations in the Indian Ocean, the Far East, Australasia and the west coast of North America, as well as to Bahrain, Dubai, Amsterdam, Frankfurt, London-Gatwick, Manchester, Paris, Rome and Zürich.
Fleet: 8 x Boeing 747-200B, 3 x 747-200F, 6 x 747-300, 6 x 747-400, 13 x Lockheed L1011 TriStar 1, 4 x L1011 TriStar 100
On order: 10 x Airbus A330, 1 x Boeing 747-200F, 7 x 747-400, 2 x 747-400F

Colour scheme: A broad mid-green cheatline, widening towards the front, is trimmed below in white and separates the grey underside from the white upper fuselage. Bold red Cathay Pacific titles appear on the front cabin roof, alongside the symbol of the Swire Group which owns the airline. The green tail has two 'streamlining' bands below a small Union flag.
Illustrated: Cathay's fleet is built around the Boeing 747 which first entered service with the airline in May 1980. Deliveries of the latest 747-400 commenced in September 1989.

Channel Express (LA/EXS)

Established: January 1978
Base: Bournemouth International Airport, Christchurch, Dorset, UK
Services: Daily scheduled cargo flights between Bournemouth and the Channel Islands, together with general cargo charter flights throughout Europe, including the carriage of newspapers, bloodstock, livestock and dangerous goods. Post Office mail flights to East Midlands, Bristol, Liverpool, Edinburgh, Luton and Guernsey. Night express parcel services are flown for leading overnight parcels companies from various points in the UK to their European distribution hubs.
Fleet: 1 x Handley Page HPR7 Herald 400, 6 x HPR7 Herald 200, 1 x Fokker F27-600 Friendship, 4 x Lockheed L188C Electra
Colour scheme: The white overall fuselage features twin cheatlines in green, the upper broader and both starting in a pencil point. Channel Express titles in green appear on the forward fuselage and on the tailfin, the first letter 'n' carrying the Rose of Sarnia.

China Airlines (CI/CAL)

Established: 16 December 1959
Base: Chiang Kai-shek International Airport, Taipei, Taiwan
Services: Regional and international passenger services from Taipei to Hong Kong, Bangkok, Phuket, Kuala Lumpur, Singapore, Seoul, Manila, Jakarta, Denpasar, Nagoya, Tokyo (Haneda), Fukuoka, Okinawa, Honolulu, Los Angeles, San Francisco, New York, Anchorage and Amsterdam. Domestic services from Taipei to Kaohsiung, Hualien and Makung. Also all-cargo flights to Dubai and Luxembourg.
Fleet: 5 x Airbus A300-600R, 6 x A300B4-200, 3 x Boeing 737-200 Advanced, 4 x 747-200B/(SCD), 3 x 747-200F, 3 x 747-400, 4 x 747SP

On order: 1 x Airbus A300-600R, 2 x Boeing 747-400, 4 x McDonnell Douglas MD-11
Colour scheme: A patriotic cheatline of red, white and blue, runs the length of the fuselage, dividing the grey underside and white upper fuselage. Large blue and red fin flashes take up most of the tail. Blue titling on the cabin roof reads China Airlines in both English and Chinese characters. Dynasty Cargo lettering in red is added at the rear to all cargo aircraft. The company motif, which does not appear on the aircraft, signifies a plum flower which is the national flower of Taiwan.
Illustrated: China Airlines' Boeing 747-200Fs fly all-cargo services to the Middle East and Europe.

Illustrated: The Handley Page Herald high-wing monoplane is now rare in Europe, but Channel Express has the largest fleet in service and is a familiar sight on the Channel Islands route.

Continental Airlines (CO/COA)

Established: 15 July 1934 as Varney Speed Lines

Base: Houston Intercontinental Airport, Houston, Texas, USA

Services: Extensive network of scheduled passenger services, both within the USA and internationally to Canada, Mexico, Australasia, Far East, and to London and Paris in Europe. Four major traffic hubs are operated at Denver, Houston, Newark and Cleveland. Domestic feeder services are provided by commuter airlines under the name of Continental Express.

Fleet: 6 x Airbus A300B4-100, 11 x A300B4-200, 13 x Boeing 727-100/C, 20 x 727-200, 79 x 72-200 Advanced, 14 x 737-100, 24 x 737-200, 55 x 737-300/LR, 2 x 747-100, 7 x 747-200B, 7 x McDonnell Douglas DC-9-14, 27 x DC-9-31/32, 7 x DC-10-10, 8 x DC-10-30, 7 x MD-81, 58 x MD-82, 2 x MD-83

On order: 11 x Airbus A300B4 x 200, 10 x A330, 10 x A340, 50 x Boeing 737-300, 50 x Embraer Brasilia

Colour scheme: Continental's latest livery was unveiled in February 1991. It has moved away from the strong and attractive gold and red which will be seen for some time yet. The new scheme is based on blue, white and gold, with the blue tailfin the dominant feature incorporating a stylised three-dimensional globe in white latitudes and gold longitudes. A thin gold pinstripe divides the upper white fuselage from the grey belly. Simple blue Continental titles are carried on the forward cabin roof.

Illustrated: The Airbus A300B4 carries up to 270 passengers in Continental's two-class service. It was the first aircraft in the fleet to be presented in the new livery.

CSA Czechoslovak Airlines (OK/CSA)

Established/First Service 19 July 1923/28 October 1923

Base: Ruzyne Airport, Prague, Czechoslovakia

Services: Extensive intra-European flights together with long-haul services from Prague to Bangkok, Bombay, Kuala Lumpur, Singapore, Jakarta, Abu Dhabi, Dubai, Damascus, Cairo, Montreal, New York, Havana and Mexico City. Domestic services link Prague, Bratislava, Piestany, Ostrava, Karlovy Vary, Kosice, Tatry and Sliac.

Fleet: 2 x Airbus A310-300, 9 x Ilyushin Il-62/M, 11 x Tupolev Tu-134A, 7 x Tupolev Tu-154M, 6 x Yakovlev Yak-40K

Colour scheme: The fresh white overall paint scheme is complemented by the red and blue colours, which make up the national flag. Pencil thin red and blue cheatlines run between large red 'CSA' initials (standing for the Czech title of Ceskoslovenske Aerolinie) and blue Czechoslovak Airlines lettering. The airline is fortunate in having the international registration prefix of 'OK' which is displayed in bold red on the tail. A blue arrow is fitted into the 'K' to provide continuation with the trailing edge of the fin.

Illustrated: The long-haul Ilyushin IL-62M four-engined airliner heads CSA's Soviet fleet, which has now been joined by the Airbus A310 the airline's first new Western aircraft. *Peter J. Cooper*

Cyprus Airways (CY/CYP)

Established/First Service: 24 September 1947/6 October 1947

Base: Larnaca International Airport, Larnaca, Cyprus

Services: Scheduled international passenger services within Europe and the Middle East, linking Larnaca with Amman, Athens, Bahrain, Birmingham, Brussels, Cairo, Damascus, Dubai, Frankfurt, Geneva, Helsinki, Jeddah, Kuwait, London, Manchester, Munich, Paris, Rhodes, Riyadh, Rome, Salonica, Tel Aviv and Zürich. Some destinations are also served from Paphos. Also charter flights.

Fleet: 4 x Airbus A310-200, 4 x Airbus A320-200, 3 x BAC One-Eleven/500

On order: 4 x Airbus A320-200

Colour scheme: The new livery introduced in late 1990 features twin 'straight through' cheatlines of royal blue and sunshine yellow below window level, separating the upper white from the lower grey fuselage. Cyprus Airways titles are promoted in blue on the mid-cabin roof. The tailfin displays the airline's white winged mountain goat symbol on a royal blue field, topped by two yellow bars and one blue bar.

Illustrated: Cyprus Airways was one of five launch customers for the Airbus A310, powered by IAE V2500 turbofan engines

Dan-Air London (DA/DAN)

Established: 21 May 1953
Base: London-Gatwick Airport, Crawley, West Sussex, UK
Services: Domestic and European scheduled services and holiday charter flights to the Mediterranean resorts and the Canary Islands. Scheduled European destinations include Amsterdam, Berlin, Berne, Gothenburg, Ibiza, Innsbruck, Lourdes/Tarbes, Madrid, Mahon, Montpellier, Nice, Oslo, Paris (CDG), Perpignan, Saarbrücken, Toulouse, Zürich and Vienna. Domestic route points incorporate Aberdeen, Inverness, London (Heathrow and Gatwick), Manchester, Newcastle, Teesside and Jersey.
Fleet: 10 x Boeing 727-200 Advanced, 4 x 737-200 Advanced, 2 x 737-300, 3 x 737-400, 2 BAC One-Eleven 200, 1 x One-Eleven 300, 11 x One-Eleven 500, 6 x HS 748, 2 x BAe 146-100, 2 x 146-300
On order: 2 x Boeing 737-400
Colour scheme: Dual dart cheatlines in the blue and red colours of the Union flag originate at the nose and fan out along the fuselage and upwards over the tail, where they enclose a white circle with the company's black and red compass and pennant shipping motif. Blue italic Dan-Air London titles are promoted on the upper fuselage alongside the Union flag.
Illustrated: The most modern aircraft in Dan-Air's fleet is the twin-engined Boeing 737-400. Fitted out for 170 passengers, it first entered service with the airline in 1988.

Delta Air Lines (DL/DAL)

Established/First Service 1924/17 June 1929

Base: Hartsfield International Airport, Atlanta, Georgia, USA

Services: Vast domestic passenger network from five main hubs and services to Canada, Mexico, Europe and the Far East. Points in Europe and the Far East include Amsterdam, Bangkok, Dublin, Frankfurt, Hamburg, Hong Kong, London-Gatwick, Munich, Nagoya, Paris, Seoul, Shannon, Stuttgart, Taipei and Tokyo. An extensive feeder network to domestic operations is provided by several commuter airlines under the 'Delta Connection' banner.

Fleet: 129 x Boeing 727-200 Advanced, 59 x 737-200 Advanced, 13 x 737-300, 69 x 757-200, 15 x 767-200, 22 x 767-300, 9 x 767-300ER, 22 x Lockheed L1011 TriStar 1, 1 x L1011 TriStar 250, 6 x L1011 TriStar 250, 11 x L1011 TriStar 500, 35 x McDonnell Douglas DC-9-32, 91 x MD-88, 6 x MD-11

On order: 57 x Boeing 737-300,13 x 757-200, 8 x 767-300, 3 x 767-300ER, 18 x McDonnell Douglas MD-88, 50 x MD-90 30, 9 x MD-11

Colour scheme: A dark blue windowline is topped by a thin red pinstripe and merges with the extended black nose radome. Black Delta titles sit above the pinstripe on the white cabin roof. The main point of interest is the large blue and red delta on the fin, and a smaller version behind the cockpit, known affectionately as the 'widget'.

Illustrated: The MD-11 trijet is the latest in a long line of Douglas aircraft operated by Delta in its impressive history. It entered service late in 1990.

DLT (DW/DLT)

Established: 1958 as OLT Ostfriesische
Lufttaxi
Base: Rhein-Main Airport, Frankfurt,
Germany
Services: Scheduled internal German
services, together with European flights
to Amsterdam, Bergen, Basle, Bastia,
Birmingham, Bologna, Brussels,
Budapest, Copenhagen, Florence,
Geneva, Glasgow, Gothenburg, Graz,
Guernsey, Jersey, Linz, Milan, Nice,
Paris, Prague, Rome, Toulouse, Trieste,
Turin, Venice, Verona, Vienna and Zürich.
Routes fan out from Frankfurt, Berlin,
Cologne, Düsseldorf, Hamburg,
Hannover, Stuttgart and Munich.

Fleet: 16 x Fokker 50
On order: 13 x Canadair Regional Jet
Colour scheme: A simple livery
distinguished by a deep blue tail over an
overall white fuselage. DLT titles appear
in blue forward of the passenger door,
and in white on the blue tailfin.
Illustrated: DLT operates a large fleet of
the 50-seat Fokker 50 twin turboprop
aircraft serving 47 destinations
throughout Europe. Other aircraft which
can be seen in DLT markings, but owned
and operated by partner airlines, are the
Dash-8 of Contactair and Tyrolean
Airways, the Saab 340 of Delta Air, and
the ATR-42 of Cimber Air and NFD.

Egyptair (MS/MSR)

Established/First Service: 7 June
1932/July 1933
Base: Cairo International Airport,
Heliopolis, Cairo, Egypt
Services: Passenger and cargo services
throughout the Middle East and to the
Far East, Africa, the USA and Europe.
Cities on the European network include
Athens, Barcelona, Berlin, Brussels,
Copenhagen, Düsseldorf, Frankfurt,
Geneva, Helsinki, Istanbul, Larnaca,
London, Madrid, Milan, Munich, Paris,
Stockholm, Vienna and Zürich. Domestic
flights link Cairo to Abu Simbel,
Alexandria, Aswan, Hurghada, Luxor and
New Valley.
Fleet: 2 x Airbus A300-600/R, 7 x A300B4-
200, 2 x Boeing 707-320C, 7 x 737-200
Advanced, 2 x 747-300, 3 x 767-200ER,
2 x 767-300ER

On order: 8 x Airbus A300-600R, 7 x
A320-200, 6 x A321, 5 x Boeing 737-
500, 2 x 767-300ER, 5 x Fokker 100
Colour scheme: A broad red windowline
runs straight through from nose to tail,
accompanied by a narrower line in gold.
Black Egyptair titles are applied in
English and Arabic either side of the
national flag. Horus, the falcon-headed
solar god of Egyptian mythology is
depicted on the white tailfin in red and
black on a gold 'sun' disk, and repeated
on the engines.
Illustrated: This Airbus A300B4 was the
third to join the fleet when it was
delivered in August 1981. It is fitted out
for 255 passengers in first class and
economy class configuration. *Peter J.
Cooper*

L AL Israel Airlines (LY/ELY)

Established/First Service: 15 November 1948/August 1949

Base: Ben Gurion International Airport, Tel Aviv, Israel

Services: Scheduled passenger and cargo services dominated by European connections and extending to the USA, Canada and Africa. European points include Amsterdam, Athens, Brussels, Bucharest, Budapest, Cologne, Copenhagen, Frankfurt, Geneva, Istanbul, Lisbon, London, Madrid, Manchester, Marseille, Munich, Rome, Stockholm, Vienna, Warsaw, Zagreb and Zürich.

Fleet: 3 x Boeing 707-320B/C, 2 x 737-200 Advanced, 1 x 747-100 (SCD), 8 x 747-200C/F, 3 x 757-200, 4 x 767-200 (ER)

Colour scheme: The white fuselage is bisected by an unusual cheatline arrangement at window level, starting with bright blue and changing into a dark blue wedge in-line with the wing leading edge. The upper rear fuselage continues the bright blue colouring across most of the tailfin which is crowned by the Israeli flag. Prominent EL AL titling in black on the forward fuselage is interspersed with the Hebrew equivalent in gold.

Illustrated: The 224-passenger Boeing 767-200 was first delivered to EL AL in July 1983.

Emirates (EK/UAE)

Established/First Service: May 1985/25 October 1985

Base: Dubai International Airport, Dubai, United Arab Emirates

Services: Scheduled passenger and cargo flights throughout the Middle East and to destinations in Europe and Asia, serving Amman, Bandar Abbas, Bangkok, Bombay, Cairo, Colombo, Damascus, Delhi, Dhaka, Frankfurt, Hong Kong, Istanbul, Jeddah, Karachi, Kuwait, London-Gatwick, Male, Manchester, Manila, Riyadh, Singapore and Tehran.

Fleet: 3 x Airbus A300-600R, 2 x A310-300, 3 x Boeing 727-200 Advanced

On order: 1 x Airbus A300-600R, 3 x A310-300, 2 x A330

Colour scheme: A vast representation of the red, white and green United Arab Emirates flag flies upwards from the rear fuselage to cover most of the tail, providing the only flash of patriotic colours on the overall white fuselage. Gold Emirates roof titles are displayed in English and Arabic, with the latter also appearing on the engine cowlings.

Illustrated: The Airbus is the flagship of the Emirates fleet, presently numbering five aircraft with seating capacities ranging from 181 to 261 passengers in a three-class configuration.

thiopian Airlines (ET/ETH)

stablished/First Service: 26 December
1945/8 April 1946
ase: Bole International Airport, Addis
Ababa, Ethiopia
ervices: Flag services from Addis Ababa
to points throughout Africa and to Abu
Dhabi, Aden, Athens, Beijing, Berlin,
Bombay, Dubai, Jeddah, London,
Moscow, Rome and Sana'a. Also vital
domestic flights to more than 40
destinations.
eet: 2 x ATR42, 3 x Boeing 707-320C, 3
x 727-200, 1 x 737-200, 2 x Boeing 757-
200, 3 x 767-200, 8 x Douglas DC-3, 1 x
DHC-5A Buffalo, 5 x DHC-6 Twin Otter
300, 2 x Lockheed L100-30 Hercules

On order: 2 x Boeing 757-200
Colour scheme: The livery is dominated
by three attractive tail feathers in the
national colours of green, yellow and red.
These are complemented by a similarly
coloured intricate cheatline which begins
with a bright red lightning bolt at the
cockpit windows and ends in a ribbon
effect under the horizontal tailplane. The
rampant lion has been retained on the
forward fuselage. Red Ethiopian lettering
is displayed in English and Amharic, the
official local language.
Illustrated: The Boeing 767-200 is
scheduled to the airline's African
destinations as well as its main routes to
Frankfurt, London and Bombay.

Federal Express (FM/FDX)

Established/First Service: 1972/17 April 1973

Base: Memphis International Airport, Memphis, Tennessee, USA

Services: Scheduled air cargo and express freight delivery services now covering 85 countries across the globe from major sorting hubs at Memphis, Newark, Oakland, Brussels and London.

Fleet: 104 x Boeing 727-100F/C, 30 x 727-200F Advanced, 9 x 747-100F, 11 x 747-200B/F, 40 x Cessna 208A Caravan I, 178 x 208B Caravan I Super, 11 x Fokker F27-500 Friendship, 8 x F27-600, 6 x McDonnell Douglas DC-8-73F, 11 x DC-10-10F, 16 x DC-10-30F

On order: 28 x Boeing 727-200F Advanced, 24 x Cessna 208B Caravan I Super, 6 x Fokker F27-500, 8 x McDonnell Douglas MD11F

Colour scheme: The unusual livery is dominated by a distinctive shade of purple which covers the entire top half of the fuselage, including the leading edge and top part of the fin. It contrasts sharply with the white half of the aircraft from which it is separated by a narrow red pinstripe. White Federal titles forward of the wing are reversed out of the purple and applied above red Express lettering which forms part of the pinstripe. The company livery was created by Richard Runyon Design of Los Angeles.

Illustrated: A line-up of McDonnell Douglas DC-10 freighters illustrates the well-known 'Fedex' colours. The DC-10s have now been joined by the newer and larger MD-11.

Finnair (AY/FIN)

Established/First Service: 1 November
1923/11 February 1924

Base: Helsinki-Vantaa Airport, Helsinki,
Finland

Services: Long-haul routes to Toronto,
Los Angeles, New York, Bangkok
Singapore, Beijing and Tokyo, together
with a European network serving
Amsterdam, Athens, Berlin (Tegel),
Brussels, Budapest, Copenhagen,
Frankfurt, Geneva, Gothenburg,
Hamburg, Istanbul, Leningrad, Lisbon,
London, Madrid, Malmo, Milan, Moscow,
Munich, Oslo, Paris, Prague, Rome,
Stockholm, Stuttgart, Tallinn, Vienna,
Warsaw and Zürich. Domestic flights are
also undertaken.

Fleet: 5 x ATR72, 2 x Airbus A300B4-200,
1 x Boeing 737-200C, 5 x McDonnell
Douglas DC-10-30/ER, 1 x MD-11, 5 x
DC-9-41, 12 x DC – 9-51, 5 x MD-82, 5 x
MD-83, 3 x MD-87

On order: 3 x McDonnell Douglas MD-11,
4 x MD-82

Colour scheme: The aircraft livery is a
patriotic portrayal of the national colours
of white and blue, symbolising snow and
sky, and comprises a blue windowline
which runs the full length of the fuselage,
and a tail painted to represent the
Finnish flag. Attention is drawn to the
blue Finnair titles with a smart sash in
three shades of blue. A small company
emblem, the flying 'F', is applied on the
nose in white on a blue disk.

Illustrated: On 29 November 1989, Finnair
became the first airline in the world to
take delivery of the MD-11, McDonnell
Douglas' newest trijet. It first entered
service on 20 December on charter
flights to gain operational experience,
before being transferred to scheduled
long-haul services.

Garuda Indonesia (GA/GIA)

Established: 31 March 1950
Base: Kemayoran Airport, Jakarta,
  Indonesia
Services: International scheduled
  passenger and cargo services to several
  regional destinations and long-haul
  flights to Honolulu, Los Angeles, Abu
  Dhabi, Jeddah, Riyadh, Cairo, Rome,
  Zürich, Vienna, Frankfurt, Paris, Brussels,
  Amsterdam and London. Also an
  extensive domestic network linking
  Jakarta and 30 other points throughout
  the Indonesian archipelago.
Fleet: 9 x Airbus A300B4-200, 5 x Boeing
  737-300, 6 x 747-200B, 6 x Fokker F28-
  3000 Fellowship, 28 x F28-4000, 15 x
  McDonnell Douglas DC-9-32, 6 x DC-10-
  30
On order: 9 x Airbus A330, 12 x Fokker
  100, 9 x McDonnell Douglas MD-11

Colour scheme: One of the smartest
  airline liveries, it was designed by Walter
  Landor Associates of San Francisco and
  unveiled in September 1985. Its centre
  piece is a modern representation of the
  'garuda', the sacred bird of Hinduism,
  which is displayed on the deep-blue fin
  in progressive shades from blue to
  turquoise. The five 'wing feathers'
  symbolise the five national ideals. The
  garuda also appears alongside dark blue
  Garuda Indonesia titling on the all-white
  fuselage. The national flag is painted
  above the first cabin windows.
Illustrated: The Boeing 747-200B serves
  all Garuda's long-haul routes from
  Jakarta. First introduced in summer
  1980, its six aircraft are fitted out for 39
  passengers in a three-class layout.

GB Airways (GT/BGL)

Established: 1931 as Gibraltar Airways
Base: London-Gatwick Airport,Crawley, West Sussex, UK
Services: Scheduled services from London-Gatwick to Casablanca, Tangier, Gibraltar, Tunis, Funchal and Jerez de la Frontera, Oviedo and Seville. Also from Manchester to Gibraltar with a through-service to Tangier. Charters to points in Europe and the Mediterranean area.
Fleet: 3 x Boeing 737-200 Advanced
Colour scheme: Broad blue and red cheatlines at window level and below run the length of the all-white fuselage,

dropping near the front to form a 'chin strap'. At the change of direction, the cheatlines incorporate a red diamond motif from the Bland Group which founded the airline. This is repeated on the tailfin, again set into bands of blue and red. The current livery was created in 1988 when GB Airways consolidated its operations at London-Gatwick Airport.
Illustrated: The Boeing 737-200 now performs all the airline's flights including the short hop across the Strait of Gibraltar to Tangier in Morocco.

Ghana Airways (GH/GHA)

Established/First Service: 4 July 1958/16 July 1958

Base: Kotoka International Airport, Accra, Ghana

Services: International passenger and cargo services to Europe, serving Düsseldorf, London and Rome, and regionally from Accra to Abidjan, Banjul, Conakry, Cotonou, Dakar, Freetown, Harare, Lagos, Lome, Monrovia and Las Palmas. Also domestic services linking the capital with Kumasi, Sunyani and Tamale.

Fleet: 1 x Fokker F28-2000 Fellowship, 1 x F28-4000, 1 x McDonnell Douglas DC-9-51, 1 x DC-10-30

Colour scheme: Based on the national tricolour, the aircraft are distinguished by a broad cheatline in red, yellow and green which widens at the base of the tail. The company insignia, comprising a black star – the symbol of African freedom – and red, yellow and green wings, is carried on the white centre engine of the DC-10 surmounted by a large national flag. Black Ghana Airways titles are displayed on the mid-upper fuselage.

Illustrated: The Fokker F28 Fellowships make up half of the Ghana Airways fleet. First delivered in July 1974, they serve domestic points and neighbouring West African destinations.

ulf Air (GF/GFA)

tablished/First Service: 24 March
950/5 July 1950
\se: Muharraq International Airport,
\ahrain
rvices: Intercontinental route network of
0 destinations in 31 countries,
xtending from the Middle East into
\urope, East Africa, the Indian sub-
ontinent, the Far East and Australasia.
\ addition to many points in the Middle
\ast, the route system includes Athens,
\angkok, Bombay, Cairo, Colombo, Dar-
\s-Salaam, Delhi, Dhaka, Frankfurt,
\long Kong, Istanbul, Karachi, Khartoum,
\arnaca, London, Manila, Nairobi, Paris,
\ingapore and Sydney.
\et: 10 x Boeing 737-200 Advanced, 9 x
\67-300ER, 8 x Lockheed L1011 Tristar
00/200

On order: 12 x Airbus A320-200, 3 x
Boeing 767-300ER
Colour scheme: The livery features the
national colours of the four states,
Bahrain, Qatar, Oman and the United
Arab Emirates. A maroon, green and red
'chin' flash leads the all-white fuselage,
above which appear English and Arabic
Gulf Air titles in gold lettering. Vertical
maroon, green and red bands, separated
by thin white stripes, also colour the top
half of the tail, below which flies a golden
falcon, symbolic of the Arabian
peninsula.
Illustrated: The Lockheed TriStar, which
has been in service since 1976,
continues to fly some of the airline's
main routes. *Peter J. Cooper*

Hamburg Airlines (HX/HAS)

Established: 15 April 1988
Base: Fühlsbuttel Airport, Hamburg, Germany
Services: Regional services connecting Hamburg, the north German trade capital, with major European business centres including Brussels, Amsterdam and Rotterdam. Domestic flights are also operated from Hamburg to Berlin, Dresden and Leipzig, in addition to services between Berlin and Saarbrücken and Münster/Osnabrück.
Fleet: 3 x DHC-8-100, 2 x DHC-8-300

Colour scheme: A smart livery comprising a dark blue windowline highlighted by a red pinstripe, which runs the full length of the fuselage, broken at the rear by HAMBURG airlines titles in blue and red. The largely blue tail with a similar red pinstripe, displays the airline's emblem of an upward flying aircraft in white, enclosed in a white circle outline.
Illustrated: The two models of the Boeing de Havilland twin-engined DHC-8 'Dash 8' regional aircraft in the fleet, are fitted out for 36 and 48 passengers respectively.

HeavyLift Cargo Airlines (NP/HLA)

Established: 31 October 1978
Base: London-Stansted Airport, Stansted, Essex, UK
Services: Cargo charter and contract services specialising in the carriage of outsize and bulky freight anywhere in the world. Major market areas are Europe, North America, Africa and Australasia. Also aircraft maintenance and spares holdings at Southend Airport.
Fleet: 1 x Boeing 707-320C, 1 x Conroy CL-44-0 Guppy, 3 x Lockheed L100-30 Hercules, 5 x Shorts SC5 Belfast
Colour scheme: The livery is dominated by a highly visible white 'H' casting a

blue shadow across the all-red fin towards the leading edge. The white upper and grey lower fuselage is divided by a dark blue cheatline at window level beneath two pinstripes in red and blue. The cheatline arrangement is interrupted twice by HeavyLift titles in blue and red at the front and rear of the aircraft.
Illustrated: HeavyLift is operating the Lockheed Hercules alongside two aircraft unique to the airline, the Conroy CL-44-0 Guppy and the massive ex-Royal Air Force Shorts Belfast (seen in the background).

Iberia (IB/IBE)

Established: 7 July 1940

Base: Barajas Airport, Madrid, Spain

Services: International flag services to all major European destinations and to North, Central and South America, Africa, the Middle East and Far East, serving almost 100 points in nearly 50 countries. Also extensive domestic scheduled and European leisure flights mainly through a number of subsidiary companies, including Aviaco, Binter, Cargosur and Viva Air.

Fleet: 8 x Airbus A300B4-100/200, 2 x A320-200, 35 x Boeing 727-200 Advanced, 7 x 747-200B/SCD, 8 x McDonnell Douglas DC-10-30, 28 x DC-8-32/33F, 15 x MD-87

In order: 20 x Airbus A320-200, 8 x A321, 8 x A340, 16 x Boeing 757-200, 9 x McDonnell Douglas MD-87

Colour scheme: A bright sunshine livery successfully combining the red and gold colours of the national flag with an allusion to the country's holiday attraction. Triple cheatlines of red, orange and gold, sweep down from behind the cockpit and along the fuselage at and above the windowline. White italic Iberia titles are set into the red and orange bands of the cheatline. A cleverly quartered 'IB' logo in red and gold on the white tail carries a royal crown.

Illustrated: The three-engined Boeing 727-200 still makes up the largest number of aircraft in the Iberia fleet. The type first entered service with the Spanish national carrier in May 1972.

Icelandair (FI/ICE)

Established/First Service: 3 June 1937/4
 May 1938
Base: Reykjavik Airport, Reykjavik, Iceland
Services: International scheduled services
 to Amsterdam, Baltimore/Washington,
 Copenhagen, Faroe Islands, Frankfurt,
 Glasgow, Gothenburg, Hamburg,
 Helsinki, Kulusuk Island, London,
 Luxembourg, Narssarssuak, New York,
 Orlando, Oslo, Paris, Reykjavik (Keflavik),
 Salzburg, Stockholm and Vienna.
 Domestic flights link 10 points with the
 capital Reykjavik.
Fleet: 3 x Boeing 737-400, 2 x 757-200ER,
 5 x Fokker F27-500
On order: 1 x Boeing 737-400, 1 x 757-
 200ER, 3 x Fokker 50

Colour scheme: The scheme displays th
 traditional Icelandic colours of white an
 blue in a striking, yet simple fashion. A
 conventional 'straight-through'
 windowline in mid-blue is trimmed by a
 similarly-coloured pinstripe below, and
 contrasted by black Icelandair lettering
 above. A small Icelandic flag appears o
 the forward fuselage. The company's
 symbol, a heavily stylised, flowing 'F' –
 standing for Flugleidr, its Icelandic nam
 – adorns the white tail.
Illustrated: Flagship of the fleet is the
 twin-Rolls-Royce powered Boeing 757
 200ER, introduced on its transatlantic
 routes in May 1990. It is configured for
 22 'Saga' Business Class and 167
 Economy Class passengers. *Peter J.
 Cooper*

nter European Airways (IEA) (IP/IEA)

stablished/First Service: 1986/1 May
1987
ase: Cardiff-Wales Airport, Rhoose,
Glamorgan, Wales, UK
ervices: Holiday charter flights to the
Mediterranean and North African resort
areas from Cardiff, Bristol, Belfast,
Manchester, Newcastle, Birmingham,
Glasgow and Luton. Specific winter
flights serve Salzburg, Munich, Geneva
and Grenoble.
eet: 3 x Boeing 737-300, 1 x 757-200

Colour scheme: The aircraft wear the
corporate colours of red, sunshine yellow
and brown of the parent company, Aspro
Holidays. Two pairs of red and yellow
cheatlines flow at a low level from the
nose along the white fuselage, which
contrasts with brown undersides. The
cheatlines sweep up the rear of the tail
where they are surmounted by black IEA
initials in a modern typeface. Full Inter
European roof titling is employed in a
similar style.
Illustrated: As with many other holiday
airlines, the Boeing 737-300 is an ideal
size for Inter European's Mediterranean
charters.

Iran Air (IR/IRA)

Established: February 1962

Base: Mehrabad Airport, Tehran, Islamic Republic of Iran

Services: Scheduled passenger and cargo services to Abu Dhabi, Athens, Bombay, Damascus, Dubai, Doha, Frankfurt, Geneva, Istanbul, Karachi, Kuala Lumpur, Larnaca, London, Paris, Beijing, Rome, Sharjah, Tokyo and Vienna. Domestic cargo flights serve Bandar Abbas and Shiraz.

Fleet: 5 x Airbus A300B2-200, 4 x Boeing 707-320C, 2 x 727-100, 4 x 727-200 Advanced, 3 x 737-200/C Advanced, 1 x 747-100, 2 x 747-200B (SCD), 1 x 747-200F, 4 x 747SP, 6 x Fokker 100

Colour scheme: A blue windowline is underscored by a blue pinstripe, both running the full length of the white upper fuselage. At the rear the blue broadens at the base of the tail and is repeated at the top to form a flowing and distinctive fin design. In between flies the Homa, a mythical bird of ancient Persia symbolising good fortune and great strength. It is the traditional symbol of Iran Air. Small Iran Air The Airline of the Islamic Republic of Iran titles on the forward cabin roof are headed by the Iranian flag. The basic colour scheme was introduced in 1962.

Illustrated: The Fokker 100 is the smallest and newest aircraft type in the Iran Air fleet. It entered service in August 1990.

aqi Airways (IA/IAW)

stablished/First Service: December
1945/29 January 1946

ase: Saddam International Airport,
Baghdad, Iraq

ervices: Scheduled regional and long-
aul services in Middle East and to
Europe, the Far East, North Africa and
South America. European points are
Amsterdam, Athens, Belgrade, Berlin,
Brussels, Bucharest, Budapest,
Copenhagen, Frankfurt, Geneva,
stanbul, Larnaca, London, Madrid,
Moscow, Paris, Prague, Rome, Sofia,
Vienna and Warsaw. Also small domestic
network Many international services are
still suspended as a result of the Gulf
War.

eet: 5 x Antonov An-12, 6 x An-24, 3 x
Boeing 707-302C, 6 x 727-200
Advanced, 2 x 737-200C Advanced, 3 x

747-200C, 2 x Dassault Falcon 20F, 3 x
Falcon 50, 32 x Ilyushin Il-76M/MD, 6 x
Lockheed L1329 JetStar II, 4 x Piaggio
P166-DL2

Colour scheme: A bright green cheatline
at window level is topped by a dark
green fuselage roof, which tapers at the
'waist' and sweeps up to encompass the
tail. The company's bird motif, believed
to date from Mesopotamian times, flies
in a white disk on the fin. White Iraqi
Airways and Iraqi titles are carried in
English and Arabic on the forward
fuselage and tail respectively, on the
starboard side; and vice versa on the
port side.

Illustrated: The three Boeing 747-200Cs
head a mixed Boeing fleet which
operates alongside Soviet equipment.

Japan Airlines (JAL) (JL/JAL)

Established/First Service: 1 August
1951/25 October 1951
Base: Narita Airport, Tokyo, Japan
Services: International passenger and
cargo services worldwide, except to
Africa, together with high-density, high-
frequency domestic flights linking Tokyo
with 14 major Japanese cities. European
destinations are Amsterdam, Athens,
Berlin, Copenhagen, Düsseldorf,
Frankfurt, London, Madrid, Milan, Paris,
Rome and Zürich.
Fleet: 12 x Boeing 747-100/F, 30 x 747-
200B/F, 13 x 747-300, 10 x 747-400, 3 x
767-200, 13 x 767-300, 15 x McDonnell
Douglas DC-10-40
On order: 30 x Boeing 747-400, 10 x
McDonnell Douglas MD-11
Colour scheme: JAL has recently
introduced a new corporate image to
replace that which has been in use since
the introduction of its Boeing 747 aircraft

in 1970. The new design, which was
developed by Walter Landor Associates
of San Francisco, features a fusion of the
JAL letters with a red square and grey
band. JAL's 'Tsuru', a stylised version of
a traditional family crest using the crane,
an auspicious bird in Japan, has been
retained on the tail of the aircraft, but
with the new stylised JAL replacing the
previous lettering. The straight-standing
black JAL letters are designed to
express dedication and reliability. The
red square symbolises the further
strengthening of the JAL corporation,
with the burning enthusiasm of youth
and energy. They grey band indicates a
sense of vibrancy and the spirited and
speedy stance taken by JAL in meeting
the challenges of the future.
Illustrated: Japan Airlines is the largest
Boeing 747 operator. Its fleet totals 65
aircraft, with a further 30 on order.

AT Yugoslav Airlines (JU/JAT)

Established: 1 April 1947

Base: Belgrade Airport, Belgrade, Yugoslavia

Services: Extensive network of scheduled passenger services within Yugoslavia and to 50 cities in Europe, the Middle East, the Far East, Australia and North America. Also charter flights through its subsidiary Air Yugoslavia and general aviation activities such as agricultural work.

Fleet: 3 x ATR42-300, 1 x Antonov An-12(F), 8 x Boeing 727-200 Advanced, 9 x 737-300, 4 x McDonnell Douglas DC-10-30, 9 x DC-9-32

In order: 2 x McDonnell Douglas MD-11

Colour scheme: The national colours of red, white and blue feature strongly, especially on the tail fin displaying the traditional white JAT logo in a red oval field, which has remained virtually unchanged since the airline's foundation. Yugoslav Airlines and 'Jugoslovenski Aerotransport' titles are applied on the cabin roof of the largely white fuselage. The starkness of the white is softened by a dramatic 'chin strap' of blue, red and silver which wraps around the front fuselage.

Illustrated: The Boeing 727-200 Advanced still forms an important part of JAT's short/medium-haul fleet for services within Europe and to the Middle East.
Peter J. Cooper

Jersey European Airways (JY/JEA)

Established: 1979
Base: Exeter Airport, Exeter, Devon, UK
Services: Domestic services to Belfast
City Airport, Birmingham, Blackpool,
Bournemouth, Bristol, Exeter, Guernsey,
Jersey, London-Stansted, Manchester,
Isle of Man and Southampton, together
with flights to Dinard and Paris in France.
Fleet: 8 x Fokker F27-500, 1 Shorts 360
Advanced
Colour scheme: The new livery, designed
by Dan Ranger and introduced in late
1990, is dominated by the airline's new
symbol appearing on the forward
fuselage and on the tailfin of the almost

totally white aircraft. It comprises
diagonal stripes of colours, graduating
from red via orange to primrose yellow
and finishing in mid-blue, the whole
forming a dynamic and aspirational delta
shape. Jersey European titles run along
the lower fuselage in blue. The italic
serif-faced Lectura suggests movement
and is expanded for maximum visibility.
Illustrated: Jersey European has now
standardised its fleet on the Fokker F27
Friendship, having recently acquired a
batch of aircraft from Australia,
previously operated by East-West
Airlines. *Austin J. Brown via JEA*

Kenya Airways (KQ/KQA)

Established/First Service 22 January 1977/4 February 1977

Base: Embakasi Airport, Nairobi, Kenya

Services: Regional and European schedules from Nairobi and Mombasa serving London, Paris, Frankfurt, Zürich, Rome, Copenhagen, Athens, Cairo, Khartoum, Jeddah, Dubai, Muscat, Bombay, Addis Ababa, Mogadishu, Seychelles, Zanzibar, Dar-es-Salaam, Entebbe, Kigali, Bujumbura, Lusaka, Lilongwe, Johannesburg and Harare. Domestic routes serve Nairobi, Mombasa, Malindi and Kisumu.

Fleet: 3 x Airbus A310-300, 3 x Boeing 707-320B, 1 x 720B, 3 x Fokker 50, 2 x Fokker F27-200, 1 x McDonnell Douglas DC-8-71

On order: 3 x Boeing 757-200

Colour scheme: A triple cheatline in the national colours of black, red and green runs along the fuselage, with the red central windowline extended at the front up to the cockpit windows. Black Kenya Airways titles are carried on the white cabin roof, together with the Kenyan flag. Stylised KA initials are painted on the tail in red within a black circle.

Illustrated: Flagship of the Kenya Airways fleet is the Airbus A310 which serves all European cities on the scheduled network.

KLM Royal Dutch Airlines (KL/KLM)

Established /First Service: 7 October 1919/17 May 1920

Base: Schiphol Airport, Amsterdam, The Netherlands

Services: International passenger and cargo services to almost 150 cities on all continents. Through its subsidiary, KLM Cityhopper, formerly NLM and Netherlines, services link Amsterdam, Rotterdam, Eindhoven and Maastricht to several cities in France, Belgium, Germany and the UK.

Fleet: 10 x Airbus A310-200, 2 x Boeing 737-200, 13 x 737-300, 13 x 747-300(SCD)/300M(SUD), 8 x 747-400/(SUD), 6 x McDonnell Douglas DC-10-30

On order: 5 x Boeing 737-400/500, 2 x 747-400/F, 10 x McDonnell Douglas MD-11

KLM Cityhopper: 4 x Fokker F27-200 Friendship, 3 x F27-500, 4 x F28-4000 Fellowship, 5 x Fokker 50, 8 x Saab 340B

On order: 5 x Fokker 50, 4 x Saab 340B.

Colour scheme: A deep blue windowline is flanked by a narrower white stripe below and a light-blue cabin roof above. The KLM logotype (from the Dutch name Koninklijke Luchtvaart Maatschappij) is painted in dark blue and topped by a royal crown in light blue on the all-white tailfin. The logo also appears in white on the cabin roof. Small KLM Royal Dutch Airlines titles are set forward in the lower white fuselage stripe. KLM Cityhopper aircraft have an all-white fuselage finished at the rear in blue which extends up the tail. White 'Cityhopper' titles follow the line of the leading edge of the fin, and smaller 'KLM Cityhopper' lettering is applied above the windows.

Illustrated: Most of KLM's European services are flown by Boeing 737-300 twin-engined jet aircraft.

A total of 12 34-seat Saab 340B turboprops will be in service with KLM Cityhopper when deliveries are completed in 1992.

orean Air (KE/KAL)

stablished: June 1962
ase: Kimpo International Airport, Seoul,
Korea
ervices: Extensive schedule of
international passenger and cargo
services to many regional destinations
and from Seoul to Amsterdam, Frankfurt,
London, Paris and Zürich in Europe, to
Tripoli via Bahrain and Jeddah, and to
Los Angeles, New York, Toronto and
Vancouver in North America. Also
domestic flights to Cheju, Pusan and
other smaller towns.
leet: 10 x Airbus A300-600/R, 10 x
A300B4/F4, 2 x Boeing 707-320B/C, 5 x
727-200, 7 x 727-200 Advanced, 16 x
747-200B/C/F, 3 x 747-300, 4 x 747-
400, 2 x 747SP, 1 x CASA 212-100
Aviocar, 1 x Cessna 500 Citation, 1 x
Dassault Falcon 20F, 1 x Falcon 50, 1 x
Fokker F27-500 Friendship, 3 x F28-

3000 Fellowship, 3 x McDonnell Douglas
DC-10-30, 12 x MD-82
On order: 14 x Airbus A300-600R, 30 x
Boeing 747-400, 8 x McDonnell Douglas
MD-11
Colour scheme: A pale shade of sky blue
colours the entire upper fuselage and tail
unit, below which runs a silver cheatline,
representing the sea. The company logo,
known as the 'Taeguk', combines the
red yin and blue yang symbols
representing the opposing forces of
nature – in this case, heaven and earth –
with white added to show 'endless
strength of progress'. It is promoted on
the tailfin and in place of the letter 'o' in
the Korean Air fuselage titling. This
striking livery was introduced in 1984.
Illustrated: One of Korean Air's 25 Boeing
747s takes off from Seoul's Kimpo
International Airport.

Kuwait Airways (KU/KAC)

Established/First Service: March
1954/April 1954

Base: Kuwait International Airport, Kuwait

Services: Reduced scheduled passenger
services from Cairo as a result of the
1991 Gulf War. Main route is Bombay-
Bahrain-Cairo-London Heathrow-New
York. Other points served are Karachi,
Jeddah, Dubai and Damascus.

Fleet: 3 x Boeing 727-200 Advanced, 4 x
747-200B (SCD), 1 x 767-200ER

On order: 5 x Airbus A300-600R, 3 x
A310-300, 3 x A320-200, 4 x A340-200,
3 x Boeing 747-400

Colour scheme: A broad windowline and
tail band in ocean blue, trimmed on both
sides in black, provide a bright contrast
to the white fuselage top. The
company's bird symbol flies in the tail
band, reversed out in white. Kuwait
Airways titles are applied in blue on the
cabin roof, in both English and Arabic.

Illustrated: A Boeing 727-200 Advanced
of Kuwait Airways in exile, departs from
London-Heathrow Airport in February
1991. *Peter J. Cooper*

Libyan Arab Airlines (LA/LNA)

Established/First Service: September 1964/October 1965
Base: Tripoli International Airport, Tripoli, Socialist People's Libyan Arab Jamahiriya.
Services: International passenger and cargo services, both on a scheduled and charter basis, within Africa and to the Middle East and Europe. Cities served in Europe include Athens, Amsterdam, Belgrade, Frankfurt, Istanbul, Larnaca, London, Madrid, Malta, Moscow, Paris, Rome, Sofia, Warsaw and Zürich. Also domestic flights.
Fleet: 2 x Airbus A310-200, 5 x Boeing 707-320B/C, 1 x 727-200, 9 x 727-200 Advanced, 1 x Dassault Falcon 20C, 1 x Falcon 50, 1 x Fokker F27-400 Friendship, 12 x F27-600, 3 x F28-4000 Fellowship, 2 x Gulfstream II, 1 x Ilyushin Il-76M, 18 x Il-76T/TD, 1 x Lockheed L100-30 Hercules, 1 x L1329 JetStar 8
Colour scheme: The livery is a blend of gold and chocolate brown on a predominantly white fuselage. A wide gold windowline is trimmed with brown pinstripes, as is the base of the golden tailfin. The company motif, representing a gazelle in full flight, appears in chocolate brown on a white disk. Libyan Arab Airlines titles are presented in both English and Arabic.
Illustrated: The Boeing 727-200 flies to most European and North African destinations.

Loganair (LC/LOG)

Established: 1 February 1962
Base: Glasgow Abbotsinch Airport, Paisley, Renfrewshire, UK
Services: Domestic services linking the Scottish communities of Barra, Benbecula, Campbeltown, Eday, Edinburgh, Fair Isle, Foula, Glasgow, Inverness, Islay, Kirkwall, Lerwick, North Ronaldsay, Out Skerries/Whalsay, Papa Westray, Papa Stour, Sanday, Stornoway, Stronsay, Tiree, Unst, Westray, and Wick, as well as Belfast, Blackpool, Guernsey, Jersey, Leeds/Bradford, Londonderry and Manchester. Carrickfin in the Irish Republic is also served.
Fleet: 2 x BAe 146-200, 2 x BAe ATP, 5 x Pilatus (B-N) BN-2A Islander, 3 x de Havilland Canada DHC-6 Twin Otter 300, 3 x Shorts 360, 2 x Shorts 360 Advanced.
Colour scheme: A broad red windowline, trimmed below by a narrower black stripe, runs along the all-white fuselage and sweeps up to encompass the lower half of the tail, which incorporates an elegant red and black company symbol, cleverly stylised to form the letters LA. A red Loganair title is painted above the cheatline, with small black subsidiary Scotland's Airline lettering below the black cheatline at the front.
Illustrated: The British Aerospace ATP twin-prop airliner forms part of a mixed fleet, ranging in seating capacity from 8 to 110 passengers.

LOT Polish Airlines (LO/LOT)

Established: 1 January 1929

Base: Okecie Airport, Warsaw, Poland

Services: Widespread European network extending to the Middle East and North Africa. Long-haul services reach eastwards to Delhi, Bangkok, Singapore, Beijing and Melbourne, and across the North Atlantic to Montreal, Chicago and New York. Regular charters are flown to Toronto, Los Angeles, Mexico City, Buenos Aires, Tokyo and Sydney. A comprehensive domestic route system serves Warsaw, Krakow, Katowice, Rzeszow, Wroclaw, Poznan, Szczecin and Gdansk.

Fleet: 1 x Antonov An-12B, 8 x An-24V, 2 x Boeing 767-200ER, 1 x 767-300ER, 2 x Ilyushin Il-18, 7 x Il-62M/MK, 7 x Tupolev Tu-134A, 14 x Tu-154M

Colour scheme: The aircraft livery on an all-white fuselage is centred on a large blue LOT fuselage logo (LOT is Polish for flight), which is followed by a solid cheatline, lining up with the top of the lettering. The blue fin contains the Polish flag behind the historic flying crane insignia in a white circle. The airline name appears in English on the port side and in Polish (Polskie Linie Lotnicze) on the starboard side. A blue flash of colour also extends from behind the nose to the underside of the cockpit windows.

Illustrated: The LOT fleet at Warsaw comprises both Eastern and Western aircraft types, including these Ilyushin Il-62s and the Boeing 767 and Tupolev Tu-134.

Lufthansa (LH/DLH)

Established: 6 January 1926
Base: Rhein-Main Airport, Frankfurt, Germany
Services: Extensive worldwide system of scheduled passenger and cargo services, linking Germany with 188 destinations in 82 countries throughout Europe, and in Africa, the Middle and Far East, Australasia, North America, Central and South America. Some domestic and thinner European routes are flown on its behalf by a number of German regional and commuter airlines.
Fleet: 10 x Airbus A300-600, 12 x A310-200, 7 x A310-300, 15 x A320-200, 15 x Boeing 727-200 Advanced, 40 x 737-200 Advanced, 27 x 737-300, 32 x 737-500, 16 x 747-200B/(SCD), 6 x 747-200F, 10 x 747-400/(SCD), 10 x McDonnell Douglas DC-10-30

On order: 1 x Airbus A300-600, 3 x A310-300, 32 x A320-200, 20 x A321, 15 x A340, 15 x Boeing 737-300, 8 x 747-400
Colour scheme: Centrepoint of the aircraft livery is Lufthansa's 'flying crane' symbol, which goes back to the earliest days of German aviation when it was carried by Deutscher Aero Lloyd. It is most prominently displayed in a yellow disk within a thin blue circle on the dark blue tail, and also appears under the cockpit in blue outline. Similarly coloured Lufthansa titles in Helvetica script appear on the fuselage which is coloured white from the wing-line upwards, and light grey below.
Illustrated: The Airbus A310-300 is one of several types of Airbus aircraft operated by the German flag carrier.

Luxair (LG/LGL)

Established/First Service: 1961/April 1962
Base: Findel Airport, Luxembourg
Services: Scheduled passenger services within Europe only, linking Luxembourg with Athens, Berlin, Copenhagen, Faro, Frankfurt, Geneva, Hamburg, London, Malaga, Munich, Nice, Palma, Paris, Rome, Saarbrücken, Strasbourg and Vienna. Also charter flights to the Mediterranean, as well as to South Africa for Luxavia.
Fleet: 3 x Boeing 737-200 Advanced, 1 x 747SP (leased to Luxavia), 2 x Embraer EMB-120 Brasilia, 3 x Fokker 50
In order: 4 x Boeing 737-400 or -500, 1 x Fokker 50

Colour scheme: Pale blue and white are the dominant colours of the Luxair livery. A broad blue cheatline below window level separates the upper and lower fuselage and the blue tail, promoting the company emblem in white. This consists of a stylised L-shaped arrow enclosed in an outline circle. Strong black Luxair titling in capital letters are painted on the cabin roof behind the forward passenger door.
Illustrated: The Boeing 737-200 is Luxair's flagship and operates all major intra-European routes from Findel Airport.

Maersk Air (DM/DMA)

Established/First Service: 1969/January 1970

Base: Copenhagen Airport, Dragoer, Denmark

Services: Regional European schedules from Copenhagen to Cologne/Bonn and London-Gatwick, and from Billund to Amsterdam, Brussels, London-Gatwick and Stockholm. Domestic flights serve Odense, Esbjerg, Billund, Skydstrup, Ronne, and Vagar in the Faroe Islands. Under the title of Maersk Helicopters it also undertakes helicopter flights from Esbjerg to the North Sea oil fields.

Fleet: 2 x Aérospatiale AS332L Super Puma, 1 x BAe(HS) 125-700B, 2 x Bell 212, 10 x Boeing 737-300, 8 x Fokker 50, 1 x Shorts 360

Colour scheme: The aircraft livery employs an overall base colour of light blue, with twin cheatlines below the windows in medium and dark blue trimmed in white. The seven-pointed star company logo is promoted in white within a white outline box both on the tail and the forward fuselage in front of Maersk titles.

Illustrated: The Maersk Air twin-engined fleet is headed by the Boeing 737-300 which first entered service with the airline in summer 1985. *Peter J. Cooper*

Malaysia Airlines (MH/MAS)

Established/First Service: April 1971/9
June 1971

Base: Subang International Airport, Kuala
Lumpur, Malaysia

Services: Extensive domestic and regional
services extending to Australia, New
Zealand, China, Hong Kong, Japan,
Korea, Philippines, the USA, the Middle
East and Europe. Destinations westward
include Amman, Amsterdam, Brussels,
Colombo, Delhi, Frankfurt, Istanbul,
Jeddah, Karachi, London, Madras,
Mauritius, Paris, Tehran, Kuwait,
Seychelles and Zürich.

Fleet: 5 x Airbus A300B4-200, 14 x Boeing
737-200 Advanced, 7 x 737-400, 2 x
747-200B, 1 x 747-300(SCD), 2 x 747-
400, 5 x DHC-6 Twin Otter 300, 10 x
Fokker 50, 4 x F27-500, 5 x McDonnell
Douglas DC-10-30

In order: 8 x Airbus A330, 10 x Boeing
737-400, 6 x 737-500, 6 x 747-400, 1 x
Fokker 50

Colour scheme: The modern MAS livery is
highlighted by the fresh white upper
fuselage carrying red and mid-blue
cheatlines. A trailing sweep at the rear
accentuates design symmetry and
balance. The corporate image in red and
blue, dividing equally at mid-spine,
dominates the tailfin. It retains the
essence of the Kelantan kite while
achieving a more aerodynamic posture.
Predominantly blue Malaysia titles
appear on the forward cabin roof
preceded by the national flag. Within the
unique italicised typeface, the letters 'm',
'a' and 's' bear red clippings to denote
the initials of the airline's full name.

Illustrated: Malaysia Airlines uses its
Boeing 747-300 on the European route
to Paris and Vienna via Dubai.

Malév Hungarian Airlines (MA/MAH)

Established: 26 April 1946 as Maszovlet
Base: Ferihegy Airport, Budapest, Hungary
Services: Inter-European and Near East network serving most capital cities and other major industrial and business centres. Services also extend from Budapest to Algiers, Tripoli and Cairo in North Africa. The Black Sea holiday resorts of Varna and Bourgas in Bulgaria are also served. Cargo services are operated in a joint venture with TNT between Budapest, Linz and Cologne.
Fleet: 1 x BAe 146-200QT, 3 x Boeing 737-200, 6 x Tupolev Tu-134A-3, 12 x Tu-154B-2

On order: 1 x Boeing 737-300, 2 x 767-200ER
Colour scheme: The latest livery features a sweep of blue at the rear of the clean overall-white fuselage and the tail, which carries fin flashes in the national colours of red, white and green. Blue Malév titles appear on the forward cabin roof, alongside the flag and additional smaller Hungarian Airlines lettering. The nose cone is also painted blue.
Illustrated: The predominant position of the Tupolev Tu-154B-2 as Malév's mainline aircraft is now being challenged by the Boeing 737. *Peter Zsillé*

Manx Airlines (JK/MNX)

stablished: 1 November 1982
ase: Isle of Man (Ronaldsway) Airport,
Ballasalla, Isle of Man, UK
ervices: Year-round scheduled services
between Ronaldsway Airport and
London-Heathrow, Manchester,
Blackpool, Liverpool, Luton, Dublin,
Belfast City Airport, Birmingham, Cardiff
and Glasgow, together with direct flights
from Liverpool to Dublin and Belfast.
There are also connections from Dublin
to Blackpool and Jersey, and from
Cardiff to Düsseldorf, Brussels, Glasgow,
Belfast, Dublin and the Channel Islands.
Summer services are flown between
Ronaldsway and Jersey (via Blackpool
and Dublin), Newcastle and
Leeds/Bradford.
eet: 1 x BAe 146-100, 3 x BAe ATP, 3 x
Shorts 360

On order: 2 x BAe Jetstream 31
Colour scheme: The livery is dominated
by the island's triangular three legs motif
(an ancient symbol of the swift-travelling
sun) in white on a red field, which is a
representation of the national flag. Twin
bands of light green above dark green
(incorporating the words, in white,
'Skianyn vannin' near the front) flow
along the white fuselage, with the dark
green also colouring the tail. Manx titles
in dark green are carried on each side
near the passenger door, and also on the
tail. All lettering is a representation of a
Manx Gaelic script.
Illustrated: The airline's three 60-seat BAe
ATPs are scheduled mainly on the routes
between the Isle of Man and London and
Liverpool.

Martinair Holland (MP/MPH)

Established: 24 May 1958
Base: Schiphol Airport, Amsterdam, The Netherlands
Services: Worldwide cargo charter flights, principally over the Europe-Far East 'corridor' via the Middle East, and to Australia, Mexico and the USA. Also passenger inclusive-tour services from Amsterdam, mainly across the North Atlantic.
Fleet: 2 x Airbus A310-200(C), 2 x Boeing 747-200C(SCD), 2 x 767-300ER, 1 x Cessna 404 Titan II, 2 x Cessna 550 Citation II, 3 x McDonnell Douglas DC-10-30CF, 2 x MD-82

On order: 4 x Boeing 767-300ER
Colour scheme: A warm red windowline runs the full length of the fuselage, terminating at an angle just short of the horizontal tailplane. A stylised red 'M' shaped into an arrow, dominates the white fin. Black Martinair Holland titles, the former in a more prominent bolder typeface, are displayed on the upper fuselage.
Illustrated: Martinair's two Airbus A310s have been in service since 1984. One is in an all-passenger configuration with 247 seats, the other is a Combi variant.

MEA Middle East Airlines (ME/MEA)

Established/First Service: May 1945/20 November 1945

Base: Beirut International Airport, Beirut, Lebanon

Services: Scheduled passenger and cargo services from Beirut to destinations throughout the Middle East, North and West Africa and Europe. Points served in Europe include Ankara, Athens, Brussels, Copenhagen, Frankfurt, Geneva, Istanbul, London, Madrid, Milan, Nice, Paris, Rome and Zürich.

Fleet: 8 x Boeing 707-320C, 4 x 720B, 3 x 747-200B

In order: 3 x Boeing 757-200

Colour scheme: A red cheatline under the windows, trimmed by red pinstripes below, separates the upper white fuselage from the natural metal underside. While the pinstripes start from the aircraft nose, the broader cheatline starts some way along the fuselage behind red New Q lettering. The red tailfin incorporates a stylised green cedar on a white field, enclosed in a red circle. The cedar of Lebanon, mentioned in the Bible, symbolises strength, holiness and eternity. Prominent red MEA lettering is carried forward of the wing.

Illustrated: MEA operates the new quiet (New Q) Boeing 707 on all its international services. Its 747s are leased out. *Peter J. Cooper*

Monarch Airlines (OM/MON)

Established/First Service: 1 June 1967/5 April 1968

Base: Luton Airport, Luton, Bedfordshire, UK

Services: Extensive charter flights and IT packages from Luton, London-Gatwick, Manchester and Glasgow to Europe and the Mediterranean area, as well as long-haul flights to such destinations as the USA, Bahamas, Mexico, Brazil, Kenya, Malaysia and Thailand. Also scheduled 'leisure' routes from Luton to Mahon (Menorca), Malaga, Malta, and to Tenerife in the Canary Islands. Licences are held to serve Las Palmas, Palma de Mallorca and Alicante.

Fleet: 2 x Airbus A300-600R, 9 x Boeing 757-200/ER, 9 x 737-300

On order: 2 x A300-600R, 1 x Boeing 767 300ER

Colour scheme: Golden yellow and black 'straight-through' cheatlines contrast sharply with the predominantly white fuselage and tail, which carries the company's crowned 'M' insignia. Bold black Monarch titles appear behind the forward passenger door.

Illustrated: Monarch Airlines operates the only UK-registered Airbus A300 aircraft. Its A300-600R features the highest density seating of this particular type, carrying 361 single-class passengers on inclusive-tour operations.

Nationair Canada (NX/NXA)

Established: 19 December 1984

Base: Montreal-Mirabel Airport, Montreal, Quebec, Canada

Services: International passenger and cargo charter flights predominantly to the USA, Central America and the Caribbean, South America and Europe. Also a scheduled trans-Atlantic service from Montreal to Brussels.

Fleet: 3 x Boeing 747-100, 2 x 757-200, 4 x McDonnell Douglas DC-8-61, 2 x DC-8-62, 2 x DC-8-63

Colour scheme: Simple red Nationair titles appear on the white fuselage and complement the grey and red logo built around the initial 'N'.

Illustrated: Nationair's long McDonnell Douglas DC-8-61 is seen here at London-Gatwick. *Peter J. Cooper*

Nigeria Airways (WT/NGA)

Established/First Service: 1958/1 October 1958

Base: Murtala Muhammed International Airport, Lagos, Nigeria

Services: Scheduled passenger and cargo services to destinations in East and West Africa and long-haul flights to Amsterdam, Jeddah, London, Rome and New York. All points are served from Lagos, with some flights also from Kano and Port Harcourt. Extensive domestic route network taking in all key cities.

Fleet: 4 x Airbus A310-200, 3 x Boeing 707-320C, 8 x 737-200 Advanced, 2 x McDonnell Douglas DC-10-30

On order: 6 x ATR42-300

Colour scheme: The livery uses the green and white colours of the national flag, which itself appears vertically on the white tail, superimposed with the airline green 'flying elephant' symbol. Twin green cheatlines either side of the windows start at the centre point of the nose and run through to the rear fuselage. Bold Nigeria Airways lettering in the same green sits on top of the cheatlines.

Illustrated: A McDonnell Douglas DC-10-30 is seen at Heathrow. *Peter J. Coop*

Northwest Airlines (NW/NWA)

Established/First Service: 1 August
1926/1 October 1926

Base: Minneapolis/St Paul International
Airport, St Paul, Minnesota, USA

Services: Extensive network of scheduled
passenger services within the USA,
supplemented by feeder airlines
operating under the 'Northwest Airlink'
banner, Canada, Mexico and the
Caribbean. Also trans-Pacific flights to
the Far East, and across the Atlantic to
London-Gatwick, Glasgow, Amsterdam,
Paris and Frankfurt.

Fleet: 20 x Airbus A320-200, 20 x 727-
200, 42 x 727-200 Advanced, 12 x 747-
100, 20 x 747-200B, 8 x 747-200F, 10 x
747-400, 33 x 757-200, 23 x McDonnell
Douglas DC-9-14/15, 77 x DC-9-31/32,
12 x DC-9-41, 28 x DC-9-51, 6 x DC-10-
30, 21 x DC-10-40, 8 x MD-82

On order: 80 x Airbus A320-200, 16 x
A330, 20 x A340, 6 x Boeing 747-400, 40
x 757-200

Colour scheme: The new Northwest
corporate signature was introduced in
June 1989 and focuses on a new
symbol, applied in white near the top of
the tailfin. It offers an updated rendering
of Northwest's call letters expressing the
'N' explicitly, while the 'pointer' to its left
strongly suggests the letter 'W' and
harkens a compass pointing northwest.
The importance of the red tail is
emphasised by extending the colour
over the entire top of the fuselage, above
a strong presence of grey, to
communicate a note of seriousness and
efficiency. A deep blue tapered
speedstripe underscores the grey and
offers a sleek modern look. Large
Northwest lettering in a classical
typeface in white on grey completes the
new identity.

Illustrated: Northwest's fleet of American-
built aircraft, DC-10-40 illustrated, are
being joined by Airbus A320s, which will
total 100 when all are delivered.

Olympic Airways (OA/OAL)

Established: 1 January 1957
Base: Athens International Airport, Athens, Greece
Services: Scheduled passenger and cargo services from Athens to most European capital cities, as well as to destinations in Africa, the Middle and Far East, Australia and North America. European points are Amsterdam, Brussels, Copenhagen, Düsseldorf, Frankfurt, Geneva, Istanbul, London, Lyon, Madrid, Marseille, Milan, Paris, Rome, Stuttgart, Tirana, Vienna and Zürich. Also an extensive domestic route system serving 30 destinations.
Fleet: 8 x Airbus A300B4-100, 6 x Boeing 707-320B/C, 6 x 727-200, 11 x 737-200, 4 x 747-200B

Colour scheme: The famous six Olympic rings are painted in their traditional colours on the dark blue tailfin, which is an extension of the narrow windowline. Expanded Olympic lettering, also in dark blue, is carried on the forward half of the upper white fuselage behind a national blue and white pendant.
Illustrated: The 262-seat Airbus A300B4, configured in a two-class layout, is used on the airline's principal medium-haul routes including that from Athens to London.

Pan American World Airways (PA/PAA)

Established/First Service: 14 March 1927/19 October 1927
Base: New York-John F. Kennedy International Airport, New York, USA
Services: Worldwide network of scheduled passenger and cargo services throughout the Americas, Europe, the Middle East and Indian subcontinent, and to Nairobi in East Africa. European destinations are Amsterdam, Athens, Belgrade, Berlin, Brussels, Bucharest, Budapest, Dubrovnik, Frankfurt, Geneva, Hamburg, Helsinki, Istanbul, Cracow, Leningrad, Madrid, Milan, Moscow, Munich, Nice, Nuremberg, Oslo, Paris, Prague, Rome, Stockholm, Stuttgart, Vienna, Warsaw, Zagreb and Zürich. All its European routes are likely to be sold
Fleet: 13 x Airbus A300B4-200, 7 x A310-200, 14 x A310-300, 89 x Boeing 727-200/Advanced, 2 x 737-200, 27 x 747-100, 7 x 747-200B

IA Pakistan International Airlines (PK/PIA)

stablish/First Service: 1954/7 June 1954
ase: Quaid-i-Azam International Airport,
Karachi, Pakistan
ervices: More than 40 international
destinations in Africa, Europe, the Middle
and Far East and the USA and Canada.
European destinations are Amsterdam,
Athens, Copenhagen, Frankfurt, Istanbul,
London, Manchester, Moscow, Paris and
Rome. A 35-point domestic network is
also flown.
leet: 8 x Airbus A300B4-200, 3 x A310-
300, 5 x Boeing 707-320C, 6 x 737-300,
8 x 747-200B/(SCD), 2 x DHC-6 Twin Otter
300, 13 x Fokker F27-200, 1 x F27- 400

Colour scheme: The livery makes good
use of the national colours of green and
white, enhanced by a gold windowline
above a broad green band extending the
length of the fuselage. Pakistan
International titles in green alongside
their Urdu equivalent in gold, are
displayed on the upper forward fuselage.
White PIA initials highlight the all-green
tailfin.
Illustrated: The PIA fleet of Boeing 747-
200Bs, used on all long-haul services,
includes two Combi convertible
passenger/freight versions. *Peter J.
Cooper*

olour scheme: Introduced from 1985,
the livery is strikingly simple with huge
Pan Am titles taking up half of the mostly
white fuselage. The heavy lettering has
been provided with fins to give the
impression of forward flight. The historic
globe symbol in blue and white with Pan
Am lettering across the equator, fills the
tail, surmounted by the American flag.
ustrated: A Pan American Airbus A310-
200 pictured at a wintry London-
Heathrow Airport before the airline sold
its routes to United. *Peter J. Cooper*

Philippine Airlines (PR/PAL)

Established/First Service: 25 February 1941/15 March 1941

Base: Ninoy Aquino International Airport, Manila, Philippines

Services: International passenger and cargo services to a number of regional destinations, across the Pacific to Honolulu, San Francisco and Los Angeles, and westward to Karachi, Dubai, Dhahran, Riyadh, Bahrain, Rome, Paris, Frankfurt, Amsterdam and London. Also vast domestic network linking Manila with more than 40 other points in the 7,000 Philippine islands.

Fleet: 9 x Airbus A300B4-200, 6 x Boeing 737-300, 7 x 747-200B, 6 x BAC One-Eleven 500, 5 x HS 748-2, 10 x Fokker 50, 2 x McDonnell Douglas DC-10-30, 7 x Shorts 360-300

Colour scheme: The present livery was unveiled towards the end of 1986 and combines a stylish all-white fuselage finish with succinct solid blue Philippine titling on the forward fuselage. The blue, white and red 'interlocking triangle' tail design inspired by the Philippine flag, features a sun bursting spectacularly from the red. The eight rays of the sun, also adopted from the flag, signify the first eight provinces to revolt against Spain during the independence movement in 1898.

Illustrated: Philippine Airlines uses its fleet of Airbus A300B4s on high-density regional routes. *Marcel Walther/WAF News*

Qantas Airways (QF/QFA)

Established: 16 November 1920

Base: Sydney Kingsford Smith Airport, Mascot, New South Wales, Australia

Services: International scheduled passenger and cargo services from Sydney and other state capitals to cities in New Zealand, the South Pacific, South East Asia, Japan, Zimbabwe, Canada, the USA, Argentina and Europe. Services to Europe take in Rome, Frankfurt, Manchester and London.

Fleet: 16 x Boeing 747-200B/SCD, 6 x 747-300EUD, 8 x 747-400, 2 x 747SP, 7 x 767-200ER, 6 x 767-300ER

On order: 6 x Boeing 747-400, 6 x 767-300ER

Colour scheme: The new Qantas image is the work of Sydney design consultants Tony Lunn and Associates, and was officially unveiled in June 1984. It features an all-white fuselage with a strong tailfin arrangement in which the warm red is extended down around the fuselage. The red fin is trimmed in gold at the leading edge for added elegance and sophistication. The white kangaroo symbol has been retained albeit somewhat larger and without wings to help strengthen the design. The tail shape has been designed into triangular logos for the engine cowlings. Black Qantas titles in classic Helvetica typeface are displayed near the forward passenger door, complemented by additional The Spirit of Australia wording below, also in black. On the Boeing 747-400 service, the name Longreach is painted in gold on each side of the nose, and the upturned wingtips – known as winglets – are in red with a gold edge.

Illustrated: The Qantas Boeing 747-400 streaks into the sky to carry the Spirit of Australia around the world.

RFG Regionalflug (VG/RFG)

Established: 1976
Base: Dortmund Wickede Airport, Dortmund, Germany
Services: Cross-border routes from Dortmund to London-Gatwick and Lyon, together with internal services to Frankfurt, Stuttgart, Nuremberg and Munich. With the exception of Nuremberg, those are also served from Paderborn/Lippstadt. Tourist flights are operated to Jersey, Guernsey, Bastia, Olbia, Florence, Malta, Rimini and Rijeka.
Fleet: 4 x ATR42-300/(QC), 4 x Swearingen SA226TC Metro II

Colour scheme: Two-tone blue cheatlines start from the centre of the nose and extend along the all-white fuselage and up to the top of the tailfin. These are interrupted on the forward fuselage and at the centre of the tail by the RFG logo in the darker blue. The cheatline arrangement is also repeated on the engine cowlings.
Illustrated: The 46-passenger ATR42-300 twin turboprop flies RFG's main services within Europe.

Royal Air Maroc (AT/RAM)

Established: 25 June 1953
Base: Casablanca-Anfa Airport, Casablanca, Morocco
Services: Scheduled passenger and cargo services to most major European destinations and to Tunis, Tripoli, Abidjan, Dakar, Conakry, Libreville, Malabo, the Canary Islands, Nouakchott, Cairo, Damascus, Jeddah, Riyadh, and across the Atlantic to Rio de Janeiro, New York and Montreal. Also domestic flights including a frequent shuttle between Casablanca and Rabat.
Fleet: 3 x ATR42-300, 2 x Beechcraft 95-B55 Baron, 2 x Super King Air 200, 2 x Boeing 707-320C, 2 x 727-200, 6 x 727-200 Advanced, 7 x 737-200/C

Advanced, 2 x 737-400, 1 x 747-200B(SCD), 1 x 747SP, 2 x 757-200
Colour scheme: A green, white and red window line separates the upper white fuselage from the grey underside. It tapers at both ends and promotes strong royal air maroc titles in lower case red. The centre piece of the national flag is the green pentangle (or seal of Solomon), which adorns the tail in the form of a shooting star, whose red trail emanates from below bold red RAM initials.
Illustrated: Royal Air Maroc's fleet consists almost entirely of Boeing aircraft. It ranges from the 707 through to the 757 and includes this three-engined 727-200.

Royal Brunei Airlines (BI/RBA)

Established/First Service: 18 November 1974/May 1975

Base: Bandar Seri Begawan, Negara Brunei Darussalam

Services: Regional passenger services to Bangkok, Darwin, Jakarta, Kota Kinabalu, Kuala Lumpur, Kuching, Manila, Singapore and Taipei, as well as to Dubai, London-Gatwick and Frankfurt.

Fleet: 3 x Boeing 757-200, 2 x 767-200ER

On order: 1 x Boeing 767-300ER

Colour scheme: Adopted in early 1986 to coincide with the delivery of its first Boeing 757, the airline's livery is based on the colours of the national flag. The design features a yellow lower fuselage separated from the white roof by pinstripes in yellow and black, and sweeping upwards over the tailfin. The national arms depicting a vertical wing support standing on the Muslim crescent, forms the main feature of the fin. Black Royal Brunei titles are worn on the cabin roof alongside the national flag.

Illustrated: The airline's all-Boeing fleet includes this 767-200ER twin-engined aircraft which flies long-haul services to Frankfurt and London.

oyal Jordanian (RJ/RJA)

stablished/First Service: 8 December
1963/15 December 1963

ase: Queen Alia International Airport,
Amman, Jordan

ervices: International passenger and
cargo services throughout the Middle
and Far East, North Africa, Europe and
the USA. European destinations include
Amsterdam, Athens, Belgrade, Brussels,
Bucharest, Copenhagen, Frankfurt,
Geneva, Istanbul, Larnaca, London,
Madrid, Malaga, Paris, Rome and
Vienna. Also domestic flights between
Amman and Aqaba.

eet: 6 x Airbus A310-300, 3 x A320-200,
3 x Boeing 707-320C, 3 x 727-200
Advanced, 6 Lockheed L1011 TriStar
500

On order: 5 x A340

Colour scheme: The present livery,
created by Walter Landor Associates of
San Francisco and introduced in 1986,
was designed to convey a spirit of
Jordan's heritage using majestic gold
and red cheatlines along a unique
charcoal grey upper fuselage. The gold
crown of the Hashemite Kingdom
dominates the tailfin, which also features
subtle tapered speed bands in dark grey
and a red tip. Royal Jordanian titles in
gold are applied along the cabin roof in
both English and Arabic.

Illustrated: The Boeing 727-200 Advanced
is used on local services in the Middle
East. *WAF News*

Royal Nepal Airlines (RA/RNA)

Established: 1 July 1958
Base: Tribhuvan Airport, Kathmandu, Nepal
Services: International scheduled flights from Kathmandu to New Delhi, Karachi, Dubai, Frankfurt and London-Gatwick, and eastward to Calcutta, Dhaka, Lhasa, Rangoon, Bangkok, Hong Kong and Singapore. Vital domestic services are provided to points on the southern slopes of the Himalayas and to isolated inland valleys totalling 39 destinations.
Fleet: 2 x Boeing 727-100, 2 x 757-200, 3 x HS748-2A/B, 10 x DHC 6 Twin Otter, 1 x Pilatus PC-6B/B1-H2 Turbo Porter

Colour scheme: A pure white fuselage conveys the snow-capped peaks of the Himalayas, crossed by twin diagonal fins bands in the national colours of red and blue, which continue on to the rear fuselage. Blue Royal Nepal Airlines titles are displayed on the forward cabin roof and preceded by the unusual 'double-triangle' flag. The company's traditional 'winged Buddha' symbol is painted beneath the cockpit windows.
Illustrated: Flagship of the Royal Nepal Airlines fleet is the Boeing 757, which is used on all long-haul services. It is pictured here at Bangkok's Dong Muan International Airport.

Ryanair (FR/RYR)

Established: 1986
Base: Dublin Airport, Dublin, Republic of Ireland
Services: Scheduled passenger flights within the Irish Republic and to points in the UK, serving Cardiff, Cork, Donegal, Dublin, Galway, Kerry, Knock, Liverpool, London-Stansted, Luton, Manchester, Shannon, Sligo and Waterford. Also from Stansted to Munich.
Fleet: 3 x ATR42-300, 1 x BAC One-

Eleven 500, 4 x Rombac One-Eleven 500
On order: 2 x Airbus A320-200, 10 x ATR42-300
Colour scheme: The livery is based on the ancient blue and gold colours of the Republic. It features an all-white fuselage with large Ryanair titles below the windows forward of the wing, and an interlinked triple 'R' symbol on the tailfin
Illustrated: The ATR42-300 has been in service with the Irish carrier since 1989

Sabena Belgian World Airlines (SN/SAB)

Established: 23 March 1923
Base: Brussels-National Airport,
Zaventem, Belgium
Services: Comprehensive European and
African scheduled services network,
together with flights to the Middle and
Far East, and North America. The latest
route additions within Europe provide
new services from Brussels to Bologna,
Bristol, Cologne, Dortmund, Hamburg,
Helsinki, Munich, Norwich, Pisa,
Saarbrücken, Seville, Strasbourg,
Valencia and Vienna.
Fleet: 2 x Airbus A310-200, 1 x A310-300,
13 x Boeing 737-200/C Advanced, 6 x
737-300, 1 x 747-100(SCD), 2 x 747-300,
5 x McDonnell Douglas DC-10-30CF
On order: 5 x Airbus A340-300C, 3 x
Boeing 737-400, 11 x 737-500

Colour scheme: Classic livery promoting a
strong tail feature in the blue 'S'
bisecting a white circle on a blue tail. A
blue windowline extends along the
length of the fuselage, trimmed either
side by a narrow pinstripe in the same
colour, providing the separation of the
upper white and lower grey body.
Matching bold Sabena titles on the
forward fuselage are followed by the
Belgian flag and Belgian World Airlines in
fainter lettering.
Illustrated: Sabena has a large fleet of
Boeing 737 twin-jets which are used
extensively throughout Europe. The fleet
includes the Boeing 737-300 and the
earlier 737-200 model Illustrated.

SAS Scandinavian Airlines System (SK/SAS)

Established: 31 July 1946

Bases: Stockholm-Arlanda Airport, Stockholm, Sweden; Fornebu Airport, Oslo, Norway and Copenhagen Airport, Denmark

Services: Extensive domestic and international route system within Scandinavia and other parts of Europe, and to Africa, the Middle and Far East, the USA and South America.

Fleet: 2 x Boeing 767-200ER, 14 x 767-300ER, 22 x Fokker 50, 9 x McDonnell Douglas DC-9-21, 45 x DC-9-41, 1 x DC-10-30, 22 x MD-81, 15 x MD-82, 2 x MD-83, 12 x MD-87

On order: 2 x Boeing 767-300ER, 14 x McDonnell Douglas MD-81, 4 x MD-82, 4 x MD-87

Colour scheme: A rhombus in the national colours of the participating nations of Denmark, Norway and Sweden, in that order, provides a striking contrast to the fresh white-overall fuselage. Simple Scandinavian titling in dark blue is outlined in gold, as are the SAS initials on the tail. The three national flags appear on the rear engines or the fuselage. The SAS livery was designed by Walter Landor Associates and introduced from 1983.

Illustrated: SAS remains a prolific user of the Douglas DC-9 twinjet, as well as its successor, the MD-80 Series.

Saudia – Saudi Arabian Airlines (SV/SVA)

Established/First Service: 1945/4 March 1947

Base: King Abdul Aziz International Airport, Jeddah, Saudi Arabia

Services: Scheduled passenger services throughout the Middle and Far East, Africa, Europe and the USA. Destinations in Europe are Athens, Frankfurt, Geneva, Istanbul, Larnaca, London, Madrid, Paris and Rome, while other long-haul flights serve New York, Tokyo and Taipei. Additionally, there are scheduled cargo flights to Brussels and Milan. A 24-point domestic network is also operated.

Fleet: 11 x Airbus A300-600, 2 x Beechcraft A36 Bonanza, 19 x Boeing 737-200 Advanced, 8 x 747-100, 1 x 747-200F, 10 x 747-300, 2 x 747SP, 2 x Beechcraft King Air 100, 2 x Cessna 550 Citation II, 1 x Dassault Falcon 900, 1 x de Havilland Canada DHC-6 Twin Otter, 4 x Gulfstream II, 5 x Gulfstream III, 1 x Gulfstream IV, 17 x Lockheed L1011 TriStar 200, 1 x McDonnell Douglas DC-8-63 (leased), 8 x Piper PA-28 Archer II

Colour scheme: A double subdivided cheatline arrangement in two shades of green above two shades of blue, separated by a narrow strip of white, splits the upper white fuselage and natural metal underbelly of the aircraft. The white cabin roof promotes the Saudi flag and Saudia titles in English and Saudi Arabian Airlines lettering in Arabic on the port side, with the reverse on starboard. The all-green fin carries the Saudia insignia which consists of two swords crossed before a palm tree, based on the state arms, on a white inverted triangle, and above white Saudia lettering

Illustrated: The Lockheed TriStar 200 first entered Saudia service in summer 1975. A total of 18 were acquired, 17 of which remain in service fitted out in a three-class configuration for 214 passengers
Oliver Constant

Singapore Airlines (SQ/SIA)

Established/First Service: 28 January 1972/1 October 1972

Base: Changi International Airport, Singapore

Services: Daily flights to 36 countries linking 62 cities in Europe, the Middle East, Asia, South West Pacific, Australia/New Zealand and North America. European destinations include London, Manchester, Berlin, Brussels, Paris, Copenhagen, Amsterdam, Frankfurt, Zürich, Vienna, Rome, Athens and Istanbul. Honolulu, Vancouver, San Francisco, Los Angeles and Dallas/Fort Worth are cities served in North America.

Fleet: 6 x Airbus A310-200, 7 x A310-300, 5 x Boeing 747-200B, 1 x 747-200F, 14 x 747-300/SCD, 8 x 747-400

On order: 2 x Airbus A310-300, 27 x Boeing 747-400, 5 x McDonnell Douglas MD-11

Colour scheme: The all-white fuselage displays dramatic foreshortened cheatlines in midnight blue and yellow, below blue Singapore Airlines titles. The lower yellow 'laser' line widens to the rear and is repeated on the vertical stabiliser in order to communicate precision. A large stylised yellow bird hovers on the otherwise blue tailfin and is repeated in miniature on each engine. The corporate identity was created by Walter Landor Associates and introduced in 1972. In 1987 it was given a new logotype and modification to the colour scheme, again created by Landor Associates. The new livery is said to reflect a balance between service orientation and technical expertise.

Illustrated: Singapore Airlines currently flies eight Boeing 747-400 'Megatops' on its principal routes. If all orders and options are taken up, the fleet will eventually number 50 aircraft.

South African Airways – SAA (SA/SAA)

Established: 1 February 1934

Base: Jan Smuts International Airport, Johannesburg, Republic of South Africa

Services: International long-haul flights to Abidjan, Amsterdam, Frankfurt, Hong Kong, Lisbon, London, Manchester, Paris, Rio de Janeiro, Rome, Taipei, Tel Aviv, Vienna and Zürich, together with regional and domestic services.

Fleet: 4 x Airbus A300B2, 5 x A300B4-200, 4 x Boeing 737-200, 13 x 737-200 Advanced, 6 x 747-200B/(SCD), 2 x 747-300, 5 x 747SP

In order: 7 x Airbus A320-200

Colour scheme: The aircraft livery incorporates the orange, white and blue of the national tricolour, derived from the House of Orange. It is dominated by a distinctive bright orange tailfin from which leaps the airline's traditional winged springbok in blue, outlined in white. A broad dark blue windowline runs the full length of the white upper fuselage above a narrower line in orange. South African Airways SAA titles in blue run along the cabin roof on the port side, with Suid-Afrikaanse Lugdiens SAL wording in Afrikaans on the starboard side.

Illustrated: The Boeing 747 flies all of SAA's long-haul intercontinental services. The first of the type entered service in 1971 and the airline now operates the SP , -200, -300 and -400 models.

Swissair (SR/SWR)

Established: 16 March 1931
Base: Zürich Kloten Airport, Zürich, Switzerland
Services: Worldwide scheduled passenger and cargo network serving 109 destinations in 64 countries. The airline flies to all European capital cities except Dublin.
Fleet: 5 x Airbus A310-200, 4 x A310-300, 5 x Boeing 747-300/(SCD), 8 x Fokker 100, 10 x McDonnell Douglas DC-10-30/ER, 22 x MD-81
On order: 7 x Airbus A320, 19 x A321, 2 x Fokker 100, 12 x McDonnell Douglas MD-11, 2 x MD-81

Colour scheme: Like all Swiss airlines, Swissair is instantly recognisable by the white Holy Cross of the national flag emblazoned on a bright red tail. Bold red Swissair titles are carried on the forward white upper fuselage above twin cheatlines of brown and black below window level.
Illustrated: The Airbus A310 flies all high-density short-to-medium routes within Europe and to the Middle East and Africa.

Syrianair – Syrian Arab Airlines (RB/SYR)

Established: October 1961

Base: Damascus International Airport, Damascus, Syrian Arab Republic

Services: International scheduled passenger and cargo services to destinations within Syria and to points in Europe, North Africa, the Middle and Far East. European cities on the network include Athens, Berlin, Bucharest, Budapest, Copenhagen, Istanbul, Larnaca, London, Moscow, Munich, Paris, Prague, Rome and Sofia.

Fleet: 1 x Antonov An-24, 4 x An-26, 2 x Aérospatiale (Sud) Caravelle 10B3, 3 x Boeing 727-200, 2 x 747SP, 2 x Dassault Falcon 20F, 4 x Ilyushin I1-76M, 6 x Tupolev Tu-134B-3, 3 x Tu-154M, 6 x Yakovlev Yak-40

Colour scheme: A bright Mediterranean blue windowline trimmed with blue pinstripes above and below, extends the full length of the aircraft starting at the nose. It is surmounted by blue Syrianair titles in both English and Arabic. The company's symbol, a stylised mythical bird, flies across the sun on an otherwise blue tail.

Illustrated: Syrianair's main long-haul aircraft is the Boeing 747SP. Delivered in 1976, both aircraft are operated in a two-class format with seating for 324 passengers. *Olivier Constant*

TAP Air Portugal (TP/TAP)

Established/First Service: 14 March 1945/September 1946
Base: Lisbon Airport, Lisbon, Portugal
Services: Extensive European network and flights to Africa and North and South America. European destinations are Amsterdam, Athens, Barcelona, Basle, Brussels, Bordeaux, Copenhagen, Dublin, Frankfurt, Geneva, Hamburg, Las Palmas, London, Luxembourg, Lyon, Madrid, Manchester, Marseille, Milan, Munich, Nice, Paris, Rome, Stockholm, Stuttgart, Toulouse, Vienna and Zürich. A domestic route system includes Faro, Horta, Lisbon, Oporto, Ponta Delgada, Porto Santo and Terceira.

Fleet: 4 x Airbus A310-300, 4 x Boeing 727-200 Advanced, 9 x 737-200 Advanced, 5 x 737-300, 7 x Lockheed L1011 TriStar 500
On order: 2 x Airbus A310-300, 2 x A340, 2 x Boeing 737-300
Colour scheme: The red and white TAP logo (from Transportes Aereos Portugueses) flies up the white tail, followed by a red 'contrail' trimmed above in green, which forms the cheatline to the nose of the aircraft. Black Air Portugal titles on the cabin roof are preceded by the Portuguese flag.
Illustrated: Air Portugal's Boeing 737-200 shows off the fresh white, red and green national colours.

Tarom Romanian Air Transport (RO/ROT)

Established: 1946 as TARS

Base: Otopeni Airport, Bucharest, Romania

Services: Scheduled passenger and cargo services within Romania, and to points in Europe, Africa, the Middle and Far East, and the USA. European cities on the route system include Amsterdam, Athens, Belgrade, Berlin, Brussels, Budapest, Copenhagen, Frankfurt, Istanbul, Larnaca, Lisbon, London, Madrid, Moscow, Prague, Paris, Sofia, Vienna, Warsaw and Zürich.

Fleet: 30 x Antonov An-24, 12 x An-26, 4 x Boeing 707-320C, 4 x BAC One-Eleven 400, 7 x One-Eleven 500, 11 x Ilyushin Il-18D/V, 5 x IL-62/M, 8 x Rombac One-Eleven 500, 10 x Tupolev Tu-154B

Colour scheme: Although the airline has experimented with a number of new livery ideas, most aircraft wear a simple red scheme on a largely white fuselage consisting of the company's bird symbol enclosed in a red circle on the tailfin and red cheatlines 'straight through', made up of a windowline accompanied each side by a pin stripe. Black tarom lettering adorns the upper mid-fuselage flanked by Transportorile Aeriene Romane and Romanian Air Transport subtitles.

Illustrated: The mixed fleet of Soviet and Western aircraft includes the Tupolev Tu-154B-2 photographed at Heathrow. *Peter J. Cooper*

TAT – Transport Aerien Trans-Regional (IJ/TAT

Established: 1968
Base: St Symphorien Airport, Tours, France
Services: Large domestic network comprising radial services centred on Paris and extensive cross-country connections, together with seasonal flights to Corsica from a number of domestic and European points. Services to many European destinations are flown on behalf of Air France from Paris, Ajaccio, Bordeaux, Lyon and Marseille. In the UK, flights reach London, Bristol, Manchester, Newcastle, Edinburgh and Belfast.
Fleet: 4 x ATR42-300, 3 x Boeing 737-200C, 2 x Beechcraft 65-90 King Air, 4 x Beech 99, 6 x Beech King Air 200, 3 x de Havilland Canada DHC-6 Twin Otter 300, 9 x Fairchild FH-227B, 1 x Fairchild F-27J, 22 x Fokker F28-1000/2000/4000, 4 x Fokker 100, 3 x Swearingen SA226TC Metro II
On order: 8 x ATR42-300, 20 x ATR72, 4 x Fokker 100
Colour scheme: Blue wings set into a warm yellow field on the tailfin of the otherwise all-white aircraft are balanced by large blue TAT lettering on the forward fuselage. Smaller versions of both are displayed under the cockpit windows.
Illustrated: Latest fleet addition is the Fokker 100 twinjet used on its main routes out of Paris.

TEA – Trans European Airways (HE/TEA)

Established/First Service: October 1970/
2 June 1971

Base: Melsbroek Airport, Melsbroek,
Belgium

Services: Passenger charters and
inclusive-tour flights to all the
Mediterranean and North African holiday
destinations, and the Canary Islands.
Also now scheduled services including
Brussels-London/Gatwick. Several sister
companies have been established in
France, Switzerland, Italy and the UK.
VIP flights are undertaken by TEA
Executive Jet Services with a 12-
passenger Gulfstream III twin-engined
business jet.

Fleet: 1 x Airbus A300B1, 2 x A310-300,
19 x Boeing 737-300, 1 x Grumman
Gulfstream III

On order: 10 x Airbus A310-300, 15 x
Boeing 737-300

Colour scheme: Large TEA initials in blue
take up most of the fresh white-overall
forward fuselage, and are repeated in
white on the blue tailfin surrounded by
12 gold stars, representing the EC
countries. The striking livery was
designed by TEA in-house and
introduced in 1988.

Illustrated: The 149-seat Boeing 737-300
makes up the largest part of TEA's
modern fleet. It was introduced in 1989,
replacing the older 737-200 model.

Thai International (TG/THA)

Established: 24 August 1959
Base: Don Muang International Airport, Bangkok, Thailand
Services: Extensive regional network and services to Europe, North America, Australia and New Zealand. Cities served in Europe include Helsinki, Copenhagen, Stockholm, London, Amsterdam, Frankfurt, Munich, Vienna, Paris, Zürich, Rome, Madrid and Athens. Major routes in a comprehensive domestic system link Bangkok, Chiang Mai, Hat Yai, Nakon Ratchasima, Phuket and Surat Thani.
Fleet: 2 x ATR42-300, 2 x ATR72, 11 x Airbus A300-600/R, 14 x A300B4-100/200, 2 x A310-200, 2 x A310-300, 3 x Boeing 737-200, 3 x 737-400, 6 x 747-2 x 747-300, 4 x 747-400, 1 x BAe 146-100, 4 x BAe 146-300, 1 x McDonnell Douglas DC-8-63F, 3 x DC-10-30 ER, 2 x MD-11, 4 x Shorts 330-200, 2 x Shorts 360

On order: 5 x Airbus A300-600R, 8 x A330, 6 x B777, 4 x Boeing 737-400, 2 x McDonnell Douglas MD-11
Colour scheme: Thai's visual appearance was created by leading design consultants Walter Landor Associates and introduced in 1975. Its rich and vibrant colours vividly reflect culture and country. Opulent gold, pink and purple tones recall the gold of the temples, the brilliant hues of the orchids and the intensity of Thailand's famous shimmering silks, all incorporated in an enormous stylised orchid symbol on the tail dominating the all-white fuselage. A smaller version speeds ahead of a gold, purple, gold cheatline, which runs the whole length of the aircraft. The abbreviated purple Thai logo is displayed near the front passenger door.
Illustrated: The high-capacity Boeing 747-400 flies the airline's major long-haul routes to Europe.

Turkish Airlines (TK/THY)

Established: 20 May 1933
Base: Ataturk International Airport, Istanbul, Turkey
Services: Good coverage of European, North African, Middle East and Gulf cities, together with long-haul flights to New York, New Delhi, Bombay, Bangkok, Kuala Lumpur, Singapore and Tokyo. Domestic network includes Istanbul, Ankara, Izmir, Dalaman, Antalya, Konya, Kayseri, Adana, Gaziantep, Malataya, Diyarbakir, Van, Erzurum and Trabzon.
Fleet: 7 x A310-200, 6 x A310-300, 2 x Boeing 707-320C, 9 x 727-200 Advanced, 9 x McDonnell Douglas DC-9-30

Colour scheme: The national colours of red and white predominate on the latest scheme, with a red tailfin riding the all-white fuselage. Set into a white circle on the fin is the airline's bird symbol in red. Blue Turkish Airlines titles are preceded by a small Turkish flag, while the initials THY, standing for its name in Turkish – Turk Hava Yollari – follow nearer the rear in red.
Illustrated: THY is using the Airbus A310s on its services in Europe and to the Far East. This A310-300 model was the first to carry the new livery.

TNT International Aviation Services

Established/First Service: 1946 (in Australia)/5 May 1987 (in Europe)
Base: Windsor, Berkshire, UK
Services: Scheduled express overnight freight and cargo charter services operated by various European carriers on TNT's behalf. Scheduled destinations include Angelholm, Avignon, Barcelona, Basle, Belfast, Billund, Birmingham, Brussels, Budapest, Catania, Cologne, Copenhagen, Dublin, Forli, Frankfurt, Geneva, Genoa, Gothenburg, Helsinki, Linz, Liverpool, Lisbon, London-Heathrow, Luton, Lyon, Madrid, Malmo, Nantes, Nuremberg, Oslo, Palermo, Paris-Charles de Gaulle, Prestwick, Rome, Stockholm, Toulouse, Valencia, Vienna and Zaragoza.

Fleet: 13 x BA 146-200QT, 4 x BAe 146-300QT, 2 x Cessna Citation II
On order: 6 x BAe 146-300QT
Colour scheme: Red TNT initials in a compartmented black box on the tailfin and forward fuselage dominate the largely white-painted aircraft with a bright orange belly. Individual operators are given licence to include their logos/names on the nose area or on the engines. The TNT Malév 146-200QT operates with a regular Malév tailfin.
Illustrated: The BAe 146-200QT and -300QT (Quiet Trader) all jet-powered freighter forms the frontline fleet of TNT in Europe. All converge at night upon Cologne, the hub of its distribution services.

Transavia (HV/TRA)

Established/First Service: 1965/17
November 1966

Base: Schiphol Airport, Amsterdam, The
Netherlands

Services: Passenger flights to the
Mediterranean holiday resorts and to
Madeira and the Canary Islands,
operating a large share of the Dutch
charter market. Long-haul flights are
operated to Kenya. Scheduled
passenger services between Amsterdam
and London-Gatwick and from
Amsterdam to Las Palmas de Gran
Canarias. Sub-services are flown for
other major carriers and leasing out
aircraft also forms a sizeable part of its
business.

Fleet: 8 x Boeing 737-300, 8 x 737-
200/200C Advanced, 1 x 737-200

On order: 4 x Boeing 757-200, 6 x 737-
300

Colour scheme: Dark green stripes,
separated by pinstripes of light green,
orange and red, are headed behind the
cockpit by the initial 'T' in green outline,
with the horizontal stroke continuing the
length of the fuselage. The only other
colours on the pure white fuselage are
the Transavia titles in green, except for
the black 'T' sweeping up the tailfin, and
the Dutch flag behind the forward
passenger door. This striking livery was
introduced with the Boeing 737-300s in
early 1986.

Illustrated: Heading the Transavia fleet are
eight Boeing 737-300s configured for
149 tourist-class passengers.

Tunis Air (TU/TAR)

Established: 1948
Base: Carthage International Airport, Tunis, Tunisia
Services: International scheduled services linking Tunis with Abu Dhabi, Algiers, Amsterdam, Athens, Barcelona, Bordeaux, Brussels, Berlin, Cairo, Casablanca, Copenhagen, Dakar, Damascus, Düsseldorf, Frankfurt, Geneva, Hamburg, Istanbul, Jeddah, Khartoum, Kuwait, Lille, London, Luxembourg, Lyon, Marseille, Milan, Munich, Nantes, Nice, Palermo, Paris, Rome, Strasbourg, Toulouse, Tripoli, Vienna and Zürich.
Fleet: 1 x Airbus A320-200, 1 x A300B4-200, 8 x Boeing 727-200 Advanced, 4 x 737-200/200C Advanced

On order: 3 x Airbus A320-200, 2 x Boeing 737-500
Colour scheme: The latest livery was adopted with the introduction into service of the Airbus A320 in October 1990. It is centred on an all-white fuselage highlighted by a red flying gazelle on the tailfin. The impression of speed has been created with red pinstripes trailing down the fin and around the rear fuselage. Red Tunis Air titles in English and Arabic are displayed on the cabin roof, with the Tunisian flag near the rear.
Illustrated: The Airbus A320 is the latest addition to Tunis Air's short-to-medium range fleet of aircraft.

rans World Airlines – TWA (TW/TWA)

stablished/First Service: 13 July
1925/17 April 1926
ases: New York-John F. Kennedy
International Airport, New York
ervices: Extensive domestic trunk
services together with trans-Atlantic
flights to Europe and North Africa,
serving Amsterdam, Athens, Barcelona,
Berlin, Brussels, Cairo, Copenhagen,
Frankfurt, Geneva, Istanbul, Lisbon,
Madrid, Milan, Munich, Paris, Rome,
Stockholm, Tel Aviv, Vienna and Zürich.
leet: 11 x Boeing 727-100, 35 x 727-200,
20 x 727-200 Advanced, 14 x 747-100, 3
x 747-200, 11 x 767-200ER, 14 x
Lockheed L1011 TriStar 1, 11 x L1011
TriStar 100, 7 x L1011 TriStar 50, 7 x
McDonnell Douglas DC-9-15, 38 x DC-9-
31/32/33/34, 3 x DC-9-41, 29 x MD-82,
4 x MD-83

On order: 20 x Airbus A330-300

Colour scheme: Warm red twin cheatlines
commence at the nose, widening as they
proceed along the pure-white fuselage,
eventually wrapping around under the
rear. Solid red Trans World titles are
displayed on the forward cabin roof,
while the tailfin promotes a white TWA
logo on a rhomboid red field. The
present livery has been carried since
November 1974.

Illustrated: Trans World Airlines became
the world's second TriStar operator (after
Eastern Air Lines) when it introduced the
type into service on its St Louis-Los
Angeles route on 25 June 1972. The
TriStar still forms an important part of its
medium/long-range fleet.

United Airlines (UA/UAL)

Established: 1 July 1931
Base: Chicago-O'Hare International
Airport, Chicago, Illinois, USA
Services: Scheduled passenger and cargo
services to more than 160 cities in the
USA, Canada, Central America, Europe,
the Far East and Australasia, plus
another 70 cities served in the USA by its
United Express partners. Destinations in
Europe are London, Frankfurt, Paris and
Madrid from various cities in the USA.
Also intra-European flights from London-
Heathrow to Paris, Amsterdam, Brussels,
Frankfurt, Berlin, Hamburg and Munich.
Fleet: 24 x Boeing 727-100, 104 x 727-
200 Advanced, 48 x 737-200, 25 x 737-
200 Advanced, 101 x 737-300, 8 x 737-
500, 18 x 747-100, 2 x 747-200B, 8 x
747-400, 11 x 747SP, 26 x 757-200, 19
767-200, 15 x McDonnell Douglas DC-8
71, 46 x DC-10-10, 8 x DC-10-30
On order: 112 x Boeing 737-300/400/500,
37 x 747-400, 64 x 757-200, 16 x 767-
300ER, 34 x 777
Colour scheme: Patriotic red, white and
blue colours highlight the United livery
which features broad cheatlines in blue
and red, brightened by a third orange
band on the largely white fuselage. A
double 'U' symbol dominates the tailfin
and also appears on the forward cabin
roof in front of black United lettering.
Illustrated: The Boeing 767 twin-engined
aircraft, along with the four-engined 747
is used across the North Atlantic on
United's growing European network.

USAir (US/USA)

Established/First Service: 5 March 1937 as All-American Aviation/13 September 1937

Base: Washington National Airport, Washington DC, USA

Services: Vast domestic network connecting 120 destinations throughout the USA, plus Montreal, Ottawa, Toronto, Bermuda, Nassau, and San Juan, Puerto Rico. Trans-Atlantic flights serve London-Gatwick and Frankfurt. Several local carriers provide feeder services to domestic hubs under the USAir Express banner.

Fleet: 10 x Boeing 727-200 Advanced, 20 x 737-200, 59 x 737-200 Advanced, 92 x 737-300, 40 x 737-400, 8 x 767-200ER, 18 x BAe 146-200A, 20 x Fokker F28-1000, 25 x Fokker F28-4000, 18 x Fokker 100, 74 x McDonnell Douglas DC-9-31/32, 19 x MD-81, 12 x MD-82

On order: 12 x Boeing 737-300, 27 x 737-400, 3 x 767-200ER, 22 x Fokker 100, 20 x McDonnell Douglas MD-82

Colour scheme: A broad band of red topped by a thin deep blue cheatline, support red and blue 'USAir' titles on the forward fuselage which is finished largely in highly-polished natural metal. The deep blue fin is divided by three thin red stripes with white 'USAir' titles in the lower compartment.

Illustrated: An operator of mixture of American and European-built aircraft, this is one of USAir's Boeing 767s.

Varig Brazilian Airlines (RG/VRG)

Established/First Service: 7 May 1927/3 February 1928

Base: Galeao International Airport, Rio de Janeiro, Brazil

Services: Extensive domestic and regional scheduled passenger and cargo services, as well as intercontinental long-haul flights to destinations in Europe, West Africa, southern Africa, Japan, Mexico and the USA. European cities served are Amsterdam, Barcelona, Copenhagen, Frankfurt, Lisbon, London, Madrid, Oporto, Paris, Rome, Milan and Zürich.

Fleet: 5 x Boeing 707-320C, 10 x 727-100/C, 11 x 737-200 Advanced, 9 x 737-300, 3 x 747-200B(SCD), 5 x 747-300/SCD, 2 x 747-400, 6 x 767-200ER, 14 x Lockheed L188A/PF Electra, 12 x McDonnell Douglas DC-10-30/CF

On order: 15 x Boeing 737-300, 4 x 767-200ER, 4 x 767-300ER, 6 x McDonnell Douglas MD-11

Colour scheme: The dark blue and white livery is notable for its broad cheatline which curves round under the aircraft nose, and also features a 'seam' effect, created by two white pinstripes at window level. The airline's long-standing compass insignia is painted on the white tail above black Varig titles. These same titles are applied on the fuselage in blue alongside the Brazilian flag, and the word 'Brasil' in black. The flying figurehead motif, enclosed in an oval outline, appears either within or above the cheatline.

Illustrated: Varig's three-engined DC-10-30s fly the airline's European services, including those to London's Heathrow Airport where this aircraft was photographed.

VIASA Venezuelan International Airways (VA/VIA)

Established/First Service: January 1961/1 April 1961
Base: Maiquetia International Airport, Caracus, Venezuela
Services: Regional scheduled passenger and cargo services throughout the Americas and across the Atlantic to Amsterdam, Frankfurt, Lisbon, London, Milan, Oporto, Paris, Rome, Santiago de Compostela and Zürich.
Fleet: 2 x Airbus A300B4-200, 5 x McDonnell Douglas DC-10-30
On order: 2 x McDonnell Douglas MD-11

Colour scheme: A medium blue 'straight-through' cheatline supports blue Venezuela lettering in the middle of the fuselage and the orange VIASA logo forward, at the same time providing a division between the white upper and all-metal lower fuselage. The orange tailfin carries the VIASA logo in white and the Venezuelan flag near the top.
Illustrated: A VIASA McDonnell Douglas DC-10-30 photographed at London-Heathrow Airport in October 1990.
Peter J. Cooper

Virgin Atlantic Airways (VS/VIR)

Established/First Service June 1982/22 June 1984

Base: London-Gatwick Airport, Crawley, West Sussex, UK

Services: Scheduled value-for-money passenger services from Gatwick across the North Atlantic to New York (Newark and JFK International Airports), Boston, Miami and Los Angeles. Orlando is served on a charter basis. Services eastward currently link London with Moscow and Tokyo. Future planned routes include Singapore and Australia, with applications pending for licences to include Melbourne, Perth, Sydney and Adelaide.

Fleet: 1 x Boeing 747-100, 7 x 747-200B

Colour scheme: A simple, straight-through, windowline in orange-red divides the all-white fuselage and leads to the orange-red tailfin. The well-known Virgin signature appears in white on the fin and in a smaller red version under the cockpit windows.

Illustrated: Virgin's all-Boeing fleet of 747 can increasingly be seen at far flung destinations. Next to come on line are Singapore and Australia.

Yemenia Yemen Airways (IY/IYE)

Established: 1954

Base: El Rahaba Airport, Sana'a, Yemen

Services: International passenger flights from Sana'a and Aden to Abu Dhabi, Addis Ababa, Amman, Amsterdam, Baghdad, Bahrain, Bombay, Cairo, Damascus, Dhahran, Djibouti, Doha, Frankfurt, Istanbul, Jeddah, Karachi, Khartoum, Kuwait, Larnaca, London, Moscow, Paris, Riyadh, Rome and Sharjah.

Fleet: 2 x Boeing 707-320C, 5 x 727-200 Advanced, 3 x 737-200/C Advanced, 4 x DHC7-100, 1 x Tupolev Tu-154M

Colour scheme: The aircraft livery employs twin broad cheatlines in bright red and Royal blue, bisecting the all-white fuselage and extending upwards to fill the tailfin, where they are broken by the company motif of a wing section behind the Islamic red crescent on an oval white field. Yemenia Yemen Airways titles in blue, in both English and Arabic follow the national flag on the forward fuselage.

Illustrated: The Boeing 727-200 Advanced is the main aircraft scheduled on the airline's medium-haul routes to Europe.

ambia Airways (QZ/ZAC)

stablished: 1964
ase: Lusaka Airport, Lusaka, Zambia
ervices: Domestic and regional
scheduled passenger and cargo services
from Lusaka to Windhoek, Gaborone,
Johannesburg, Manzini, Harare,
Lilongwe, Mauritius, Dar-es-Salaam,
Nairobi, Entebbe and Bombay. Also
long-haul to London, Frankfurt and
Rome.
leet: 2 x ATR42-300, 2 x Boeing 737-200
Advanced, 1 x McDonnell Douglas DC-
10-30, 1 x DC-8-71

Colour scheme: Inspired by the national
flag, the Zambia Airways livery features
quadruple cheatlines of green, red, black
and orange at window level, separating
the white cabin roof from the grey
undersides. The green upper band
sweeps upward to encompass the entire
tail, which carries the company logo, a
Zambian eagle forming an orange 'Z' in a
similarly coloured circle. Smallish black
Zambia Airways titles appear alongside
the national flag on the forward fuselage.
Illustrated: Zambia Airways' single
McDonnell Douglas DC-10-30 trijet flies
the long-haul route from Lusaka to
Frankfurt, Rome and London.

Aircraft Nationality And Registration Marks

An organised systematic approach to the registration of civil aircraft was first proposed as early as 1912 but, due to the intervention of World War 1, it was not instituted until the Paris Air Convention in 1919. It was then recommended that all aircraft should have five letters with the first denoting the nationality. All letters were to be painted in black on white as large as possible on both sides of the fuselage as well as on the top surface and underside of the wings. In addition, the nationality letter was to be painted on each side of the tailplane. Privately-owned aircraft had to have the last four letters underlined.

As a result of the rapid development of civil aviation, almost all countries owned aircraft by 1929 and the regulations were revised accordingly. Gradually however, many of these rules were forgotten with registrations becoming smaller and the nationality letter on the tail disappearing altogether. The present standards,

adopted by ICAO on 8 February 1949, call for registrations to be applied on the upper half of the vertical tail surface. They should also be clean, clearly visible and identifiable.

With the exception of the national prefix which is adhered to by all the member nations, the individual aircraft registration is issued subject to the country's own internal regulations for civil aircraft. These are usually in the form of three or four letters (depending on whether a one or two-national prefix is allocated) either in alphabetical or numerical sequence. Some nations have their own sub-divisions which serve to group individual aircraft types and thus assist in recognition (e.g. SE-H for helicopters). In many countries, major airlines are given a special sequence which makes them instantly recognisable, such examples are ZS-SA for South African Airways, N535PA for Pan American etc.

List of aircraft nationality notified to the International Civil Aviation Organisation (ICAO)

Afghanistan	YA	Brazil	PP/P
Albania	ZA	Brunei	V
Algeria	7T	Bulgaria	L
Andorra	C3	Burundi	9‖
Angola	D2	Cameroon	T
Antigua/Barbuda	V2	Canada	‖
Argentina	LQ/LV	Cape Verde Republic	D
Aruba	P4	Cayman Islands	VR-‖
Australia	VH	Central African Republic	T
Austria	OE	Chad	T
Bahamas	C6	Chile	C‖
Bahrain	A9C	China	
Bangladesh	S2	Ciskei	(Z‖
Barbados	8P	Colombia	H
Belgium	OO	Congo, People's Republic	T‖
Belize	V3	Comoro Republic	D
Benin	TY	Costa Rica	‖
Bermuda	VR-B	Cuba	C
Bhutan	A5	Cyprus	5
Bolivia	CP	Czechoslovakia	O
Boputhatswana	(ZS)	Democratic Kampuchea	X
Botswana	A2	Denmark	O
Burkina Faso	XT	Djibouti	J

Spain	EC	AP	Pakista
Sri Lanka	4R	A2	Botswar
Sudan	ST	A3	Tonga Friendly Islan
Surinam	PZ	A40	Oma
Swaziland	3D	A5	Bhuta
Sweden	SE	A6	United Arab Emirat
Switzerland	HB	A7	Qat
Syria	YK	A9C	Bahra
Tanzania	5H	B	China (People's Republi
Thailand	HS	B	China (Taiwa
Transkei	(ZS)	C	Canac
Togo	5V	CC	Ch
Tonga Friendly Islands	A3	CCCP	Union of Soviet Socialist Republi
Trinidad and Tobago	9Y	CN	Morocc
Tunisia	TS	CP	Boli
Turkey	TC	CR/CS	Portug
Turks and Caicos Islands	VQ-T	CU	Cul
Tuvalu	T2	CX	Urugua
Uganda	5X	C2	Nau
Union of Soviet Socialist Republics	CCCP	C3	Andor
United Arab Emirates	A6	C5	Gamb
United Kingdom	G	C6	Baham
UK Colonies and Protectorates	VP/VQ/VR	C9	Mozambiqu
United Nations Organisation	4U	D	German
USA and outlying territories	N	DQ	F
Uruguay	CX	D2	Ango
Vanuatu	YJ	D4	Cape Verde Repub
Vatican	HV	D6	Comoro Repub
Venda	(ZS)	EC	Spa
Venezuela	YV	EI	Ei
Vietnam	VN	EL	Libe
Virgin Islands (British)	VP-LVA to VP-LZZ	EP	Ir
Western Samoa	5W	ET	Ethiop
Yemen	4W/70	F	Fran
Yugoslavia	YU	F-O	French Overseas Departmen
Zaire	9Q	G	United Kingdom and Channel Islan
Zambia	9J	HA	Hunga
Zimbabwe	Z	HB	Switzerland and Liechtenste
		HC	Ecuad
		HH	Ha
		HI	Dominican Repub
		HK	Colomb
		HL	Korea Repub
		(HMAY/MONGOL)	Mongo
		HP	Panar
		HR	Hondur
		HS	Thaila
		HV	Vatic
		HZ	Saudi Arab
		H4	Solomon Islan
		I	It
		JA	Jap

Notes:

A] Registration Marks shown in brackets
denote either those countries which
have become independent during the
last few years but have not yet notified
ICAO of a new Nationality Mark, or the
use of unofficial marks. Into the latter
category come (MONGOL), (HMAY) and
Vietnam (VN).

B] Arranged alphabetically in order of
nationality marks.

5B	Cyprus	7T	Alge
5H	Tanzania	8P	Barbad
5N	Nigeria	8Q	Maldiv
5R	Malagasy Republic	8R	Guya
5T	Mauritania	9G	Gha
5U	Niger	9H	Ma
5V	Togo	9J	Zaml
5W	Western Samoa	9K	Kuw
5X	Uganda	9L	Sierra Leo
5Y	Kenya	9M	Malay
6O	Somalia	9N	Nep
6V	Senegal	9Q	Za
6Y	Jamaica	9U	Burur
7O	Yemen	9V	Singapo
7P	Lesotho	9XR	Rwan
7Q	Malawi	9Y	Trinidad and Toba